ACCOUNTS OVERDUE:
Natural Resource Depreciation in Costa Rica

Raúl Solórzano
Ronnie de Camino
Richard Woodward
Joseph Tosi
Vicente Watson
Alexis Vásquez
Carlos Villalobos
Jorge Jiménez

Robert Repetto
Wilfrido Cruz

Tropical Science Center
San José, Costa Rica

World Resources Institute
Washington, D.C.

WORLD RESOURCES INSTITUTE

December 1991

Kathleen Courrier
Publications Director

Brooks Clapp
Marketing Manager

Hyacinth Billings
Production Manager

Wilfrido Cruz
Cover Photo

Each World Resources Institute Report represents a timely, scientific treatment of a subject of public concern. WRI takes responsibility for choosing the study topics and guaranteeing its authors and researchers freedom of inquiry. It also solicits and responds to the guidance of advisory panels and expert reviewers. Unless otherwise stated, however, all the interpretation and findings set forth in WRI publications are those of the authors.

Contents

Acknowledgments

This report was prepared by the Tropical Science Center (San José, Costa Rica) in conjunction with the World Resources Institute (Washington, DC).

Funding for the study was provided by the United States Agency for International Development, the International Development Research Centre (IDRC) of Canada, and the Government of the Netherlands. A start-up grant was provided by the Noyes Foundation. We also thank Vernita Fort of USAID, Frits L. Schlingemann of the Netherlands Ministry of Foreign Affairs, and David Brooks of IDRC for their wholehearted support of this project.

We wish to express our sincere gratitude to the members of the project's advisory committee for their helpful guidance and constant support, to Dr. Alvaro Umaña for his encouragement to undertake this study, and to Michael Ward for his helpful review and suggestions.

Our special thanks go as well to Eduardo Madrigal, Dirección General de Recursos Pesqueros y Acuacultura, Ministerio de Agricultura y Ganadería, for his contribution of data and suggestions, and to Javier Saborio at the Centro Agronómico Tropical de Investigacíon y Enseñanza (CATIE) for his help with the digitized maps used in this study. We also appreciate the invaluable help given by project consultants Elemer Bornemisza and Jorge Fonseca; translators Karen E. Steffensen, and Wendy Hitz; and computer programmer Hernan Badilla.

We would also like to extend our gratitude to Kathleen Lynch for her skillful editing and to Hyacinth Billings for her production coordination. Rosemary McCloskey and Lori Pierelli deserve thanks for their competent research and in-house production work, and Katy Perry for her administrative assistance.

TSC
WRI

Foreword

The UN System of National Accounts, the world's yardstick for measuring economic performance, is a flawed framework for appraising the sustainability of economic growth. While it measures how such man-made assets as factories and equipment depreciate as they are used in current production, it leaves out the effects of resource depletion and degradation. For example, national income accounts record timber output, fish harvest, and crop production as income but ignore the costs of deforestation, overfishing, and soil erosion. A nation's depletion of its natural resources—consumption of natural capital—can therefore masquerade as growth for decades, even though it will clearly reduce income prospects from resource sectors in the future. Just as ignoring the deterioration of man-made assets skews economic assessments, so does overlooking the degradation of natural assets.

The national income accounting framework is a relic of the 1930s, when raw materials were cheap and only a few visionaries could foresee the environmental threats that are common concerns today. Today's accounting framework is particularly inadequate for countries where natural resources are among the principal economic assets. In recent years, thanks in part to WRI's work on natural resource accounting, many economic analysts have endorsed the view that national accounts should be revised to treat natural resources the same way that man-made capital is treated. Until such revisions occur, policy-makers and the public will be given a misleading picture of economic performance.

Costa Rica is a case in point. In the twenty years between 1970 and 1989, the country lost natural resources worth more than one year's gross domestic product (GDP). Appropriate national income accounting methods would have recorded this 5-percent-of-GDP loss each year as depreciation of capital. Instead, the annual accounts calculated during those two decades show only a continuous rise in national income and a high rate of capital formation—right up to the crash of the 1980s. The economic crash, when it came, was called a debt crisis, but it was just as much an environmental crisis.

In *Accounts Overdue*, the Tropical Science Center in Costa Rica and the World Resources Institute collaborated to analyze the changing state of the country's forests, soils, and fisheries from 1970 to 1989. The study was set in motion when Dr. Alvaro Umaña Quesada—then Costa Rica's Minister of Natural Resources, Energy, and Mines—asked WRI to help carry out in Costa Rica a study similar to *Wasting Assets: Natural Resources in the National Income Accounts*, which was done in Indonesia. Dr. Umaña's successor, Hernan Bravo, has supported the project as strongly. Both recognize the importance for policy formation of making the economic costs of environmental degradation explicit. After two years, the project team concluded that the standard accounting system's blind spot has led Costa Rican decision-makers farther and farther from development choices that would have been economically and environmentally sustainable.

Consider just a few of the study team's findings:

- Depreciation of just three resources—forests, soils, and fisheries—amounted to more than 20 billion colones in 1989, almost 9 percent of GDP. Comparison with total capital formation is more dramatic. Natural resource depreciation exceeded one third of gross capital formation, suggesting that conventional national accounts have been overstating net asset growth by ignoring the loss of productive natural assets.

- Although steep slopes and heavy rainfall make 60 percent of Costa Rica's land suitable only for forestry, deforestation has been so rapid that it accounted for more than 85 percent of the estimated total resource depreciation for 1989. The yearly economic loss from timber cutting alone grew from 3 to more than 14 billion colones between 1970 and 1989.

- Soil depreciation amounts to almost 10 percent of Costa Rica's annual agricultural production. It averaged 2 to 3 billion colones per year throughout the study.

- While fisheries comprise only a small portion of the total economy, the loss in sustainable incomes due to resource depletion is most apparent in this sector. Given proper management, Costa Rica's main fishery in the Gulf of Nicoya would have an asset value of about 1.5 billion colones. However, over-fishing has so depleted the resource that the potential annual rents of more than 90 million colones have been dissipated, and fishermen now barely make as much as welfare recipients.

Disturbing as these findings are, they represent only a fraction of Costa Rica's actual natural resource losses. The authors measured only the loss of timber, the depletion of certain soil nutrients, and the decline of principal species in one important fishing area—leading indicators of how these three sectors are faring, but by no means the whole story. In other sectors, losses could be just as heavy.

In March 1991, the authors presented their findings at an international conference in Vancouver, British Columbia, at which more than a dozen other developing countries described their efforts to change the treatment of natural resources in their economic accounts. All called on the UN and the World Bank for a standard methodology to do this, and for technical assistance in implementing it. *Accounts Overdue* advances and complements recent WRI studies by Dr. Repetto and his colleagues, including *Wasting Assets: Natural Resources in the National Income Accounts* (Repetto et al.; 1989), *Paying the Farm Bill: U.S. Agricultural Policy and the Transition to Sustainable Agriculture* (Faeth et al.; 1991), and *The Forest for the Trees: Government Policies and the Misuse of Forest Resources* (Repetto, 1988). It also ties in with Dr. Cruz and Dr. Repetto's forthcoming study of how structural adjustment policies are affecting environment and development in the Philippines.

WRI would like to thank the governments and private entities whose generous financial support made this study possible: the United States Agency for International Development, the Netherlands' Foreign Affairs Ministry, the International Development Research Centre (of Canada), and the Jessie Smith Noyes Foundation. Our gratitude also extends to the Ford Foundation for its support of WRI's overall economic research program. To all these institutions, we express our deep appreciation.

James Gustave Speth
President
World Resources Institute

Part I. Overview and Recommendations

Background

The United Nations System of National Accounts (SNA) is the standard framework for measuring a country's macroeconomic performance. The SNA includes *stock accounts* that identify assets and liabilities at particular points in time, and *flow accounts* that keep track of transactions during intervals of time: purchases of goods and services, payments to wage and profit earners, import payments and export revenues for goods and services, for example. These national accounts have become the basis for almost all macroeconomic analysis, planning, and evaluation. Supposedly, the SNA is an integrated, comprehensive, and consistent accounting framework. Unfortunately, it is not.

Shortcomings of SNA

The present system of national accounts is a historical artifact, heavily influenced by the work of such statisticians as Simon Kuznets and Richard Stone in the 1930s and by the theories of John Maynard Keynes. It reflects the economic preoccupations of their time: the business cycle and persistent unemployment in industrial economies. Because raw material prices were at an all-time low in the 1930s, Keynesian economists paid little attention to natural resource scarcities. Consequently, the contribution that natural resources make to production and economic welfare is hardly acknowledged in the national income accounts. Capital formation is assigned a central role in economic growth theories, but natural resources are not treated like other tangible assets in the system of national accounts. Activities that deplete or degrade natural resources are not recorded as consuming capital. Nor are activities that increase the stock of natural resources defined as capital formation. According to the UN Statistical Office, "...non-reproducible physical assets such as soil or the natural growth of trees...are not included in the gross formation of capital, due to the fact that these assets are not exchanged in the marketplace" (UN, 1975).[1]

On the other hand, the SNA does classify as gross capital formation, expenses incurred in "improving" land for pastures, developing or extending timber-producing areas, or creating infrastructure for the fishing industry. SNA records such actions as contributing to recorded income and investment, although they can destroy—and in Costa Rica manifestly have destroyed—valuable natural resource assets through deforestation, soil erosion, and overfishing. (*See Part II*, this study.) This loss of capital—as natural resources are used beyond their capacity to recover—is not recorded in the income and investment accounts. The national accounts thereby create the illusion of income development, when in fact national wealth is being destroyed. Economic disaster masquerades as progress.

The national accounts create the illusion of income development, when in fact national wealth is being destroyed.

In Costa Rica, as in many other developing countries, natural resources are the most important economic asset. If sustainably managed, they generate a perpetual stream of diverse and important economic benefits. Forests, fisheries, agriculture, and mines directly contribute 17 percent of income, 28 percent of employment, and 55 percent of export earnings.[2] Yet, the System of National Accounts, recommended by the United Nations to Costa Rica and to the developing world, not only ignores the importance of these assets, but also treats their destruction as an increase in income instead of as a loss of wealth. This distortion conceals from the public and policy-makers alike the gravity of the economy's deteriorating resource base.

That Costa Rica's natural resources have deteriorated seriously is indisputable, as shown by the figures in this report. But the loss is not reflected in the national accounts. On the contrary, the net revenues from overexploiting forest, soil, fishery, and water resources is treated as factor income, not as capital consumption. Even worse, the accounting system defines the conversion of land suitable only for forests into cattle pastures as a capital investment, even if cattle ruin the soil and the livestock enterprise is neither ecologically nor economically viable.

More than 60 percent of Costa Rica's territory is suitable only for forests. Slopes are too steep, rainfall too heavy, or soils too poor for more intensive uses. Yet, at most, only 40 percent of the land remains under forest cover. By contrast, cattle pasture has spread over 35 percent of the land, when only 8 percent of it is suitable for this use.[3] This expansion of the livestock frontier is squandering the country's natural resources and is draining its financial resources as well. Banks are losing 17 billion colones annually in uncollectible loans to the cattle industry.

As things are going, Costa Rica's commercial forests will be exhausted within the next five years, and the country will be forced to import forest products. Thousands of jobs will be lost, and a source of valuable fuelwood, non-wood products, and wildlife habitat will disappear. (Flores Rodas, 1985). Meanwhile, where forests once stood, tons of soil wash away every year from dry, stripped, overgrazed pastures.

The current national accounting system serves Costa Rica poorly because it does not reflect the economic value of lost natural resources. Clearing forests for pasture is classified as investment. The loss of forest capital is simply ignored. Like the national accounts, society, and even forest owners have not recognized that the destruction of a forest today is a loss of income tomorrow. The results are devastating. Investments in unproductive pasture land are actively promoted, and the loss of forest capital is shrugged off. If the loss of potential forest income were taken into account, the true net value of conversion would often be negative—a decline in the value of the nation's assets.

Besides being conceptually flawed in its treatment of natural resources, the SNA is inconsistent. What is recognized as an economic asset in the SNA *stock* accounts is not treated as an asset in the SNA *flow* accounts. The stock accounts, or national balance sheets in the SNA, recognize land, timber, and subsoil minerals as economic assets, to be included in the national capital stock. Ironically, the UN guidelines for valuing natural resource assets in the stock accounts are entirely consistent with those used in this report. That is, the assets' market values are to be used if available; if not, the capitalized value of the stream of rents or net revenues from the asset is to be used instead. (UN, 1977.)

Logically, if a country's national balance sheets at two points in time indicate that a natural resource—say the forest—has been depleted, the flow accounts for the intervening years should show a capital consumption or depreciation allowance. If the forests have expanded, the accounts should show a corresponding amount of capital formation. This reflects perhaps the most basic identity in all of accounting: namely, that the difference in stocks between two points of time equals the net flow in the intervening period. For example, the difference in a person's net worth at the beginning and end of a year equals that person's net savings or dissavings during the year. The UN System of National Accounts violates this basic accounting identity with respect to natural resource assets.

Had Costa Rica constructed national balance sheets in 1970 and again in 1989, they would have shown that natural resource assets valued at more than one year's GDP had disappeared during those 20 years.

The inconsistency is highly misleading. Had Costa Rica constructed national balance sheets in 1970 and again in 1989, they would have shown that natural resource assets valued at more than one year's GDP had disappeared during those 20 years. Yet, in not one of those 20 years did the annual accounts of national income, expenditure, savings, and capital formation reflect that ongoing disinvestment. Instead, the accounts show only continuing growth in national income, and a high rate of capital formation, until the economy crashed in the 1980s. The national accounts gave no warning that the basis for continuing growth was being destroyed.

Even after economic crisis struck, it was labeled a ''debt crisis,'' not an environmental crisis. The International Monetary Fund rushed south with programs to stabilize the monetary situation, but nobody spoke of stabilizing the natural resource base. Yet, throughout the previous decade, the depreciation of natural resource assets, as an annual percentage of GDP, dwarfed the balance-of-payments deficit.[4] The difference was that the balance-of-payments deficit and the accumulation of external liabilities was recorded, transparent, and scrutinized. The decumulation of domestic assets went unrecorded, unnoticed, and uncorrected.

Recommendations

The idea of sustainable development, which the World Commission on Environment and Development labored to promote, is undermined by the UN System of National Accounts. In the World Commission's definition, *sustainable development* meets the current generation's needs without depriving future generations. Thus, current consumption must be matched by current earnings, without drawing down the productive assets for generating future income. Income itself, in the standard Hicksian definition, is the maximum consumption possible in the present period that does not reduce future consumption possibilities. Treating the depletion of natural resource capital as current income, as the SNA does, is inconsistent with this definition of income and incompatible with sustainable development. The UN system, as a timely and feasible contribution to the June 1992 meeting in Brazil of the UN Conference on Environment and Development, should announce that this distortion in the treatment of natural resources will be removed in the ongoing revisions to the SNA.

Costa Rica's national accounting system must also be changed so that economic policymakers no longer make misguided decisions based on inadequate and distorted information. Past failures to prevent natural resource degradation have already undermined efforts at development

3

and poverty alleviation. This linkage is still not fully recognized by policymakers, who act as if natural resources were limitless or as if technology can always replace exhausted or degraded resources. Closer dialogue between policymakers and scientists can overcome this simplistic view of the natural environment. An economic accounting system that reflects the true condition of natural resources would provide an essential tool for use in the integrated analysis of environmental and economic policies in every sector of government.

Introducing such an accounting system will require that an authoritative international institution—the United Nations—define a standard, general methodological framework. Most countries adhere closely to the current SNA to increase the international comparability of their economic statistics. In addition, an official statistical agency in Costa Rica must take responsibility for organizing data bases, and a steady flow of information to them. The methodology presented in this report can then be used to confront economic development issues realistically.

Overview of Results

The Costa Rican natural resource accounting study represents a substantial advance in methodology and data over previous efforts. Estimates of changes in forest cover, mangrove area, and other land uses were based on periodic surveys using remote sensing and satellite imaging. Data on forest type, volume, growth, and composition were based on detailed field studies using the Holdridge Life Zone classification system. Estimates of soil erosion were generated using Geographic Information System(s) (GIS) methodologies and mappings of topography, rainfall, soil type, and land use. The fishery accounts utilized scientific sampling studies of fish populations in the Bay of Nicoya. Thus, the empirical and analytical foundations of the physical accounts were detailed and systematic.

The economic analyses underlying the accounts are also relatively advanced. A detailed stumpage value model was constructed for the forestry accounts to estimate separately values for hard, soft, and medium density timber according to distance from processing mills, for each year in the period studied. For the fishery accounts, a comprehensive bioeconomic model was estimated econometrically to calculate the change in sustainable harvest levels and resource rents with increasing fishing effort. The accounts for mangrove estimate both consumptive use values (for charcoal and tanning bark) and nonconsumptive use values as habitat for mollusks and shrimp. These economic analyses also represent a significant methodological advance.

This study shows that Costa Rica has been rapidly using up its natural capital. In just two decades, from 1970 to 1989, Costa Rica's forests, soils, and fisheries have depreciated by more than 184 billion colones (US$4.1 billion).[5] (See Table I-1.) This sum exceeds the average value of one year's GDP during this period. The implications of this loss for development cannot be determined with any precision, but, in the simplest analysis, a capital loss averaging 5 percent of GDP a year could easily have reduced the potential growth rate of GDP by 1.5–2.0 percent a year.[6] Since the actual growth rate over this period averaged 4.6 percent, this would represent a 25–30 percent reduction in potential economic growth.

Because Costa Rica's forests, soils, and fisheries were exploited beyond their capacity to recover, these resources deteriorated both in quantity and quality, and their capacity to generate income was consequently diminished. The capitalized value of this income loss was quantified as the estimate of depreciation for each resource in this study. However, only part of the loss could be estimated. For forests, it was only the loss of immediate and future timber value. Other services provided by Costa Rican forests—wildlife habitat, tourist attraction, ecosystem regulator, and supplier of non-timber commodities—are important but their value has yet to be estimated. For soils, it was only the loss of principal nutrients for plant growth

Table I-1. Depreciation in Value of Costa Rica's Natural Resources (million 1984 colones)

| Year | Deforestation | | | Soil Erosion | Overfishing | Total |
	Loss of Standing Volume	Loss of Future Harvests	Growth of Secondary Forests	Total Nutrient Loss	Loss of Resource Value	
1970	2,997	214	(169)	1,940	—	4,982
1971	4,195	648	(147)	1,875	6	6,577
1972	3,279	409	(128)	1,986	7	5,553
1973	4,003	676	(110)	2,082	5	6,656
1974	4,091	934	(84)	3,180	(6)	8,115
1975	3,871	804	(61)	2,985	(16)	7,583
1976	3,212	512	(40)	2,531	(33)	6,182
1977	3,313	531	(21)	2,553	(65)	6,311
1978	3,407	548	(4)	2,350	(112)	6,189
1979	4,835	1,074	12	2,922	(93)	8,750
1980	4,356	901	26	3,088	(138)	8,233
1981	2,430	205	38	2,831	6	5,510
1982	1,854	35	49	3,120	99	5,157
1983	5,395	1,215	59	2,885	83	9,637
1984	6,010	1,439	68	3,028	166	10,711
1985	6,193	1,535	(35)	3,265	273	11,231
1986	9,224	2,575	(128)	2,497	386	14,554
1987	6,463	1,414	(212)	2,295	562	10,522
1988	14,175	4,003	(288)	2,623	650	21,163
1989	14,326	4,057	(355)	2,576	—	20,604

— Not available

Note: Figures in parentheses represent capital formation.

because of erosion. Other deleterious changes due to erosion were not captured—soil compaction, nutrient leaching, and other damage to the soil's physical and chemical condition. For fisheries, it was only the value of the principal species in one important fishing area lost through overfishing that entered the accounts. Therefore, the natural resource depreciation estimates presented in this report, large though they are, represent only a fraction of the losses that have taken place in Costa Rica.

The estimates give no reason for optimism that the losses are diminishing. In fact, during the last six years of the study period, from 1983 to 1989, the annual depreciation (in constant prices) averaged 11.2 billion colones, 70 percent greater than the average rate of 6.5 billion colones during the preceding dozen years. The increase is in part due to the increasing cost of deforestation as tropical timber becomes scarcer and more valuable.

Soil depreciation costs remained fairly constant at about 2.6 billion colones a year throughout the period. While this is considerably less than the losses of forest resources, it looms large when compared to the value of agricultural production. In a representative year, 1984, soil depreciation costs equaled 9 percent of value added in agriculture. For some extensive agricultural activities, particularly

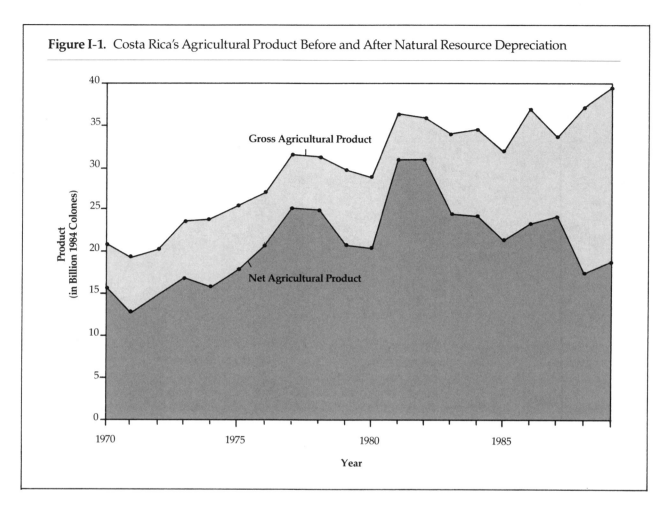

Figure I-1. Costa Rica's Agricultural Product Before and After Natural Resource Depreciation

livestock ranching, soil erosion losses represented a much larger fraction of the value of production.

The depreciation of the fishery resource, though numerically the smallest of the three sectors, is in some respects the most dramatic. The economic value of the resource was totally destroyed by unrestricted overfishing during the study period. If optimally managed, the fishery in the Gulf of Nicoya could have generated about US$2 million in annual resource rents. Instead, excess fishing pressure, mainly from underemployed rural workers displaced by economic crisis, had totally eliminated these returns by 1988. The fish biomass and the harvest both fell as fishing pressure continued to

The macroeconomic implications of resource depletion would be obvious if these resource accounts were integrated into the national income accounting framework.

increase. Artisanal fishermen, already among Costa Rica's poorest workers, by that time were earning little more than welfare payments for their efforts.

The macroeconomic implications of resource depletion would be obvious if these resource accounts were integrated into the national income accounting framework. The appropriate adjustment would be to subtract from GDP the value of resource depreciation along with the conventional capital consumption allowance (on account of tangible reproducible capital) to calculate an adjusted estimate of net domestic product. *(See Table I-2.)* Over the studied period, natural resource depreciation grew at an average rate of 6.4 percent a year. Though at the outset smaller in value than the estimated

capital consumption allowance for buildings and equipment, by 1989 natural resource depreciation had become three times as large. As a percentage of GDP, it grew from 5–6 percent in the early years to 8–9 percent in the most recent years. The growth rate of net domestic product fell from an average of 4.9 percent a year to 4.7 percent when natural resource depreciation is subtracted.

Still more drastic are changes in the investment accounts. *(See Table I-3 and Figure I-2.)* Natural resource depreciation averaged 24

Table I-2. Gross and Net Domestic Product, Net of Natural Resource Depreciation (million 1984 colones)

Year	Gross Domestic Product (GDP)	Conventional Capital Consumption Allowance (CCA)	Conventional Net Domestic Product (NDP)	Natural Resource Depreciation (NRD)	Adjusted Net Domestic Product (ANDP)	Ratio of NRD to GDP (in %)
1970	93,446	5,951	87,495	4,982	82,513	5.3
1971	94,382	5,947	88,435	6,577	81,858	7.0
1972	100,912	6,186	94,726	5,553	89,173	5.5
1973	116,525	6,503	110,022	6,656	103,366	5.7
1974	122,740	6,481	116.259	8,115	108,144	6.6
1975	125,393	6,655	118,738	7,583	111,155	6.1
1976	132,310	7,188	125,122	6,182	118,940	4.7
1977	143,990	7,394	136,596	6,311	130,285	4.4
1978	153,124	8,035	145,089	6,189	138,900	4.0
1979	160,598	8,571	152,027	8,750	143,277	5.5
1980	161,894	8,529	153,365	8,233	145,132	5.1
1981	158,237	7,511	150,726	5,510	145,216	3.5
1982	145,932	5,847	140,085	5,157	134,928	3.5
1983	154,481	5,029	149,452	9,637	139,815	6.2
1984	163,011	4,862	158,149	10,711	147,438	6.6
1985	169,299	4,694	164,605	11,231	153,374	6.6
1986	177,327	4,408	172,919	14,554	158,365	8.2
1987	186,019	4,651	181,368	10,522	170,846	5.7
1988	207,816	5,301	202,515	21,163	181,352	10.2
1989	231,289	5,323	225,966	20,604	205,362	8.9

Note: Gross Domestic Product values from Banco Central de Costa Rica (*Estadísticas 1950–1985*, San José, Costa Rica) and unpublished data were converted to constant colones. The GDP deflator used was taken from International Monetary Fund, *International Financial Statistics* 20:14 (15 July 1991). NRD is from Table I-1; ANDP is NDP less NRD.

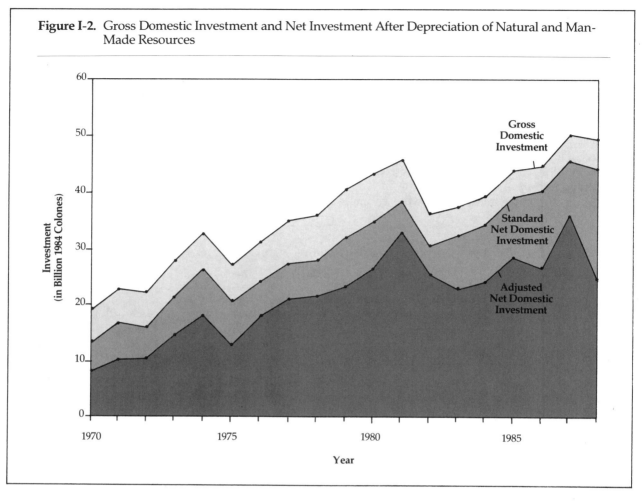

Figure I-2. Gross Domestic Investment and Net Investment After Depreciation of Natural and Man-Made Resources

percent of gross capital formation throughout the period 1970 to 1988. The conventional accounting framework thus overstated actual net capital formation in the Costa Rican economy by more than 41 percent over the period by ignoring the disappearance of Costa Rica's most productive assets—natural resources. An accounting system so misleading about an economic process as important as capital formation can be of no use for economic analysis, planning, or evaluation.

Natural resources are disappearing with increasing speed, but national policy-makers are not yet considering the implications for future economic productivity. The situation can be reversed if corrective environmental and economic policies are enacted. This is unlikely to happen unless leaders are provided with information that genuinely reflects the relationship between economic development and the natural environment and shows how the abuse of natural resources impoverishes the country. Costa Rica's wealth lies in its people, its land, its forests, and the surrounding seas. The economic ''development'' programs carried out to date have sacrificed three of these resources.

Table I-3. Gross and Net Domestic Capital Formation After Depreciation of Natural Resources (million 1984 colones)

Year	Gross Domestic Capital Formation (GDCF)	Conventional Capital Consumption Allowance (CCA)	Conventional Net Capital Formation (NCF)	Natural Resource Depreciation (NRD)	Adjusted Net Capital Formation (ANCF)	Ratio of NRD to GDCF (in %)
1970	19,191	5,951	13,240	4,982	8,233	0.26
1971	22,969	5,947	17,022	6,577	10,445	0.29
1972	22,228	6,186	16,042	5,553	10,489	0.25
1973	27,958	6,503	21,455	6,656	14,799	0.24
1974	32,819	6,481	26,338	8,115	18,223	0.25
1975	27,136	6,655	20,481	7,583	12,898	0.28
1976	31,308	7,188	24,120	6,182	17,938	0.20
1977	34,946	7,394	27,552	6,311	21,241	0.18
1978	35,925	8,035	27,890	6,189	21,701	0.17
1979	40,654	8,571	32,083	8,750	23,333	0.11
1980	43,375	8,529	34,846	8,233	26,613	0.19
1981	45,931	7,511	38,420	5,510	32,910	0.12
1982	36,212	5,847	30,365	5,517	25,208	0.14
1983	37,356	5,029	32,327	9,637	22,690	0.26
1984	39,300	4,862	34,438	10,711	23,727	0.27
1985	43,830	4,694	39,136	11,231	27,905	0.26
1986	44,704	4,408	40,296	14,554	25,742	0.33
1987	50,335	4,651	45,684	10,522	35,162	0.21
1988	49,518	5,301	44,217	21,163	23,054	0.43

Source: National Income Components; Banco Central de Costa Rica, *Estadísticas 1950–1985, División Económica,* San José; and unpublished BCCR data. Capital formation data available only up to 1988. NRD is from Table I-1; ANCF is NCF less NRD.

Part II. Costa Rica: The Detailed Natural Resource Accounts

A. Forest Accounts

Before the Spanish arrived, Costa Rica was covered with a dense cloak of deciduous forest, broken only by dispersed Indian settlements where corn, beans, cacao, cassava, and cotton were cultivated in shifting plots in the forest. The Indians, who had only stone axes, left the large trees to die off gradually as fields were cleared by burning the underbrush. Because clearing involved so much work, the fields occupied only the most fertile and least erosive alluvial soils in areas with benign climates. Because there were no cattle, the fields returned to forest after the crop cycle. The Indian population lived in harmony with the environment, obtaining meat, fish and mollusks, fruits, medicines, and building materials from forests, rivers, and oceans.

Most of the country consisted of colder hilly uplands, or infertile and poorly drained soils and excessively humid areas. Since the Indians could not use such land productively, the forests remained virgin until the conquistadors arrived. These forests varied tremendously in physiognomy, species content, and timber potential because of variations in climates, soils, and topography.

Costa Rica's Forests After the Spanish Arrival

Everything changed when the Spanish arrived. Except for a few isolated settlements in Talamanca and San Carlos, the Indians' ecologically balanced system disappeared. The Indians that survived the wars, the slavery, and frightful diseases brought from Europe interbred and adopted a Spanish culture with roots far from the humid tropics. For a long time, a small number of whites and half-breeds, culturally demoralized and isolated, lived in the interior temperate plains, practicing a simple subsistence economy. The low plains of the coasts were abandoned to malaria, pirates, and the mesquito Indians. (Thiel, 1902). In these areas, large expanses of second growth forest, originally cleared by the migrant Indians, returned uninterrupted to maturity.

It took 300 years, until the early 19th century, before Costa Rica's population recovered. Around 1822, at the time of independence, the destruction of the natural forest began again, at first slowly, as the population increased and cleared land for farms. In 1822, the population density was one person per square kilometer, and there were about 100,000 mature trees per person (Tosi, 1974, pp. 89–107). Agricultural settlement started in the Central Valley and in Nicoya—relatively fertile areas with climates suitable for many crops, but especially sugar cane, tobacco, and coffee. Coffee exports started by 1825 and in the following decades quickly grew to dominate the local economy.

Before the end of the century, the Central Valley's forests had been replaced by permanent crops, which protected the soil well. Only the finest timber, especially cedar, was used. Until 1900, the farms were stable and relatively prosperous and the regions were populous. Still, less than 10 percent of the national territory was used for crops, pastures, or other purposes. The natural forest dominated the rest.

The end of the 19th century saw a wave of spontaneous colonization toward the coasts (Sandner, 1972), especially toward the Pacific. The colonists, using European agricultural techniques, needed extensive rangelands for horses and cattle. Settlers did not stop to take account of the varying capabilities of the lands they were clearing. From valley to summit, the forests of the Puriscal, Candelaria, and Dota mountains were demolished, along with those throughout the western slopes of the Tilaran and Guanacaste Mountain Ranges.

Outside the Central Valley, extensive cattle ranches occupied large areas of land for a growing, but still sparse, population. A massive movement of landless *campesinos* spurred the deforestation of infertile soils and fragile slopes in hilly regions with high rainfall. The soils could not sustain such permanent commercial agricultural crops as coffee or sugar cane, and after a few years of subsistence crops, lands were converted into poor and eroded rangelands.

Since 1922, deforestation has increased exponentially because of official expansionist policies, very liberal land tenure laws, and high population growth rates. The 1950s gave birth to what can be called the cattle subculture. This phenomenon was encouraged by policies designed to increase beef exports, including ample credit programs funded almost entirely by international agencies. Subsidies to the beef industry were fundamental in converting Costa Rica into a large pasture, to the detriment of traditional agriculture. They also generated massive speculation for unclaimed land, which totally exhausted the supply of land in the public domain. Between 1950 and 1963, the natural forest area in the public and

private domain was diminished by 605,103 hectares, an average of 46,546 ha/yr. Between 1963 and 1973, deforestation averaged more than 48 thousand ha/yr. (*See Figure A-1,* Tosi, [1980], and data from this study.)

Deforestation during this period was due not to an expansion of cropland either for domestic consumption or for export, but almost entirely for extensive pastures that required little labor but vast area to be profitable. This "agricultural colonization" did little for poor campesinos; nor did it increase the production of basic foodstuffs for domestic consumption. It did convert the campesino into a land speculator. Landless campesinos advanced precariously over unoccupied national territory, mostly land best suited for forestry, clearing the forest with axes and fire to make the minimum "improvement" needed to assure possession. However, since obtaining legal title to the land was very difficult for the campesinos, they sold it illegally as "improved" land to wealthy buyers with bank connections, who then converted it into cattle farms.

This process was so rapid that new colonization outran the country's communication and transportation network. On the frontier, it was neither possible nor profitable to extract and sell the large volume of felled timber. More than 90 percent was converted into smoke or decomposed in the soil. This established wasteful customs that still persist among campesinos and lumbermen in Costa Rica.[7]

The Timber Economy in Costa Rica

The history of Costa Rica's forests has been one of lost opportunities and destroyed potential. Lands suitable only for forestry have long served as a land bank for the expansion of the agricultural sector and government land reform programs (*See Figure A-1*).

The timber industry in Costa Rica has been an inefficient mining operation, extracting a relatively small fraction of available timber from areas to be converted to agriculture, and selectively exploiting natural forest areas. Land use

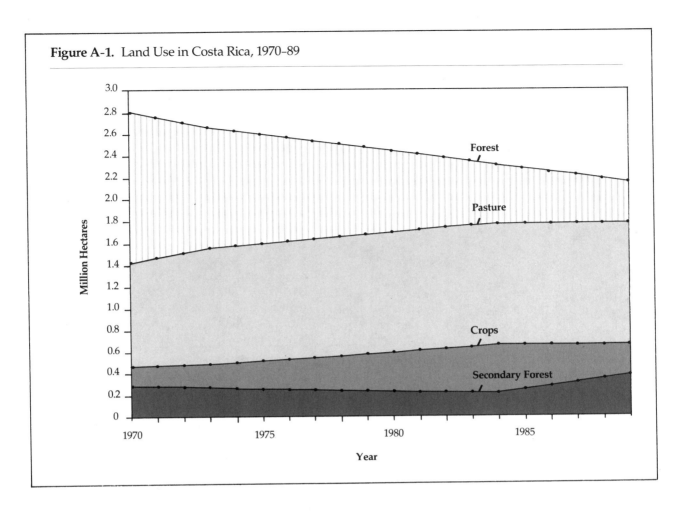

Figure A-1. Land Use in Costa Rica, 1970–89

The history of Costa Rica's forests has been one of lost opportunities and destroyed potential.

changes in most areas have been so abrupt that conversion to agriculture has taken place without even intermediate logging. Cattlemen usually arrived before loggers, directly converting the land and wasting vast quantities of timber. Where logging did take place, it was followed by land clearing for ranching, leaving no opportunity for forest regeneration. This process has been favored by the distribution of rural infrastructure, credit, legislation, and agricultural development policies (MIRENEM, 1990a).

The national forest industry's small size and low timber use are reflected in its minute contribution to agricultural gross value added and total GDP. *(See Table A-1.)* The forestry sector contribution has fluctuated between 2.9 percent and 4.0 percent of the agricultural product. Together, forestry and the forest industry sectors have contributed only between 1.48 percent and 1.91 percent of gross domestic product.[8]

13

Table A-1. Forestry's Contribution to GDP (million current colones)

Year	(A) GDP[a]	(B) Agricultural Product[a]	C) Forestry Product[b]	(D) Forest Industry Product[c]	(E) Total Forestry Product (C) + (D)	(F) Forestry As % of GDP (E) ÷ (A)	(G) Forestry As % of Ag. GDP (C) ÷ (B)
1978	30,194	6,164	189	369	558	1.8%	3.1%
1979	34,584	6,399	245	414	659	1.9%	3.8%
1980	41,405	7,372	294	480	773	1.9%	4.0%
1981	57,103	13,145	496	598	1,093	1.9%	3.8%
1982	97,505	23,884	688	767	1,455	1.5%	2.9%
1983	129,314	28,446	894	1,221	2,115	1.6%	3.1%
1984	163,011	34,572	1,365	1,706	3,071	1.9%	3.9%
1985	197,920	37,341	1,436	1,974	3,410	1.7%	3.8%
1986	246,579	51,530	2,031	2,096	4,127	1.7%	3.9%
1987	284,533	51,417	1,631	2,569	4,200	1.5%	3.2%

a. Banco Central de Costa Rica, *Estadísticas 1950–1985,* División Económica, San José, 1986; and unpublished data. Agricultural Product includes value added in the agriculture, fishery and forestry sectors.
b. Banco Central de Costa Rica, *Cifras sobre producción agropecuaria 1978–1987,* Departamento de Contabilidad Social, San José, 1989a; includes value added during extraction and transportation.
c. Banco Central de Costa Rica, *Estadísticas del sector industrial manufacturero 1978–1987,* Departamento de Contabilidad Social, San José, 1989b; includes value added through milling and the manufacturing of wood furniture.

Until 1984, the forest was generally considered an obstacle to agricultural development, and deforested land was considered more valuable than forested land. Clearing the land was thought to cost more than the timber in accessible areas was worth.[9] Elsewhere, low timber values reflected government's drive to rapidly expand the agricultural frontier: government policies caused far more trees to be cut than the timber industry could handle. Ironically, in recent years, tax incentives known as *certificados de abono forestales* (CAF), designed to encourage reforestation, have provoked a similar phenomenon. Once again generous incentives make a hectare covered with partially developed secondary forest worth less than a hectare of deforested land that can easily be replanted.[10]

The past decade has witnessed growing public support for conservation of the nation's natural resources and forests. In 1984, legislation was passed prohibiting the conversion of forest to other uses unless that land was found suitable for agricultural production. Also, a more aggressive policy to encourage forest plantations has raised the rate of reforestation from 62 ha/yr in the 1970s to 2,734 ha/yr in the 1980s (Chacón and Gamboa, 1989). Despite these changes, Costa Rica's forests are still shrinking every year.

Depreciation of Forest Resources

For timber resources, capital accounts can be expressed in physical and economic terms. In physical terms, the depreciation of a forest is equal to the net decrease in the total volume of timber from the national inventory. In this sense, the appreciation or depreciation of the forest resource *equals* the final volume of timber in a given period *less* the volume at the beginning of the period. The volume at the end of a period *equals* the initial volume *plus* the increases due to growth and new forests (plantations and secondary forests) *minus* the changes due to deforestation, exploitation, damage, and fires.

Physical depreciation of forest resources can also be expressed as the difference between the final area and the initial area of forests. Differences in surface area are produced by changes in the extent of fallow lands, secondary forests, and newly reforested areas. Nevertheless, depreciation expressed in purely physical terms, whether volume or surface area, tends to hide important differences in composition, quality, age, and value among timber stands.

The economic value of a forest's standing timber *equals* the market value of the wood *less* the costs of extraction, transport, and milling (ET&M). This value, which can be applied to a single tree or to a whole forest, is called the *stumpage* value. According to this definition, the economic depreciation of the forest asset is the difference between the stumpage value of the forest at the beginning and the end of the year. (This definition assumes unchanged prices during the year. The treatment of changes in timber prices and costs is discussed below.) In terms of loss of income-generating capacity, depreciation is equal to the decline in the present value of a forest's future profits due to harvests and land clearing. The capital value of a forest does not depreciate if the harvest (both qualitative and quantitative) does not surpass growth in the same period. But cutting in excess of growth reduces the total value of the asset and depreciates the resource.

Changes in land use from forest to agriculture imply an increase in agricultural sector assets and a corresponding decrease in forest-sector assets. The conversion of lands suitable for agriculture represents a net increase in the value of national assets, but deforestation of lands with low agricultural capacity and high forestry value results in net loss of wealth. However, the United Nations System of National Accounts (SNA) defines the clearing of lands for agriculture as capital formation, but does not define the corresponding loss of capital in the forest sector as depreciation.

The value added in logging increases national income. However, in the current system, resource rent (stumpage value) is not distinguished from the return to labor and invested capital. When harvesting surpasses growth, the part of production that exceeds growth and curtails the forest's potential is, illogically, also regarded as part of the national income instead of capital consumption. This should be changed. *Future loss* of production should be defined as *capital consumption*, as it is in this study.

So far, forest depreciation, measured either by the stumpage value or by the loss of future profits, has been defined only in terms of timber. In reality, indirect benefits, which may not have market value, should also be considered. Forests that have no direct value as timber but do have high indirect values cannot be correctly valued by the conventional accounting methods explained above.[11]

Physical Accounts

To determine the extent and nature of forest loss, Costa Rica was divided into homogeneous ecological units.

A land units map was developed by overlaying maps of bioclimate or life zones (TSC, 1990), soil groups and slopes (Vásquez, 1989), and geology (Dirección de Geología, Minas y Petróleo, 1982), all at a scale of 1:200,000. This multi-layered map, showing 860 distinct combinations called ''land units,'' was then digitized using the ERDAS system and converted to

ARC/INFO format using a program written specifically for this project (Badilla, 1990).

The land unit map was overlaid with two land use maps. One was for 1984 (IGN, 1985). The other (IGN, 1970) made use of aerial photographs from the early 1960s and some effort to ''actualize'' the areas was made when it was published in 1970. These overlays together provided a ''land use matrix'' composed of the 860 land units divided into the different uses described by each map.

Land uses for 1963 and 1973 were identified using agricultural censuses of those years and then distributed across areas by straight-line interpolation between the 1960 and 1984 land use maps. (IGN, 1970)[12]

To estimate the standing volume of timber, by type, on each land unit, the detailed field studies of distinct forest types were associated with the land units on which they occur. Timber volume and species composition were estimated comprehensively, and then adjusted downward for non-usable wood. The procedure is explained in detail in Annex A-1.

A multinational study by Brown (1984) corroborates the estimates derived by this methodology. Using data from the United Nations Food and Agriculture Organization (FAO), Brown estimated the average biomass of Latin American forests at 176 mt/ha, equivalent to a volume of 283 m³/ha of trees over 10 cm in diameter (using a mean density of 0.62 g/cm³). The present study yields an average of 360 m³/ha for the study plots, for an average of 288 m³/ha of trees over 10 cm in diameter.

Table A-2 shows volume estimates by Brown and by the present study for different life zones.

The volume differences between Latin America and Costa Rica are small. Volume is, however, slightly greater in Costa Rican forests where soil quality is better, and rainfall higher, than in Amazonian forests. (Annex A-2 shows similar results from other studies.)

Although the estimates of volume and annual growth may seem high, they are more accurate than typical forest inventory studies because they are based on scientific measurements of

Table A-2. Estimates of Tropical Forest Volumes in Latin America and Costa Rica (m³/ha, trees > 10 cm diameter)

Life Zone[a]	Latin America[b]	Costa Rica[c] Potential	Mean
Tropical moist forest	332–558	240–502	192–402
Tropical wet forest	177–479	101–986	81–789
Premontane wet forest	440–671	217–619	174–495
Premontane moist forest	102	157–200	126–160
Lower montane rain forest	620	210–963	168–770
Lower montane wet forest	435	317	254

a. L.R. Holdridge, Life Zone Ecology (San José, Costa Rica: Tropical Science Center) 1967.
b. S. Brown, ''Biomass of Tropical Forests: A New Estimate Based on Forest Volumes,'' *Science* 223 (Mar 1984):1290–93.
c. Results of this study. *See Annex Table A-1-1.*

the physiognomy of each association or type of forest in its mature state. The data are useful in determining evapotranspiration, average timber density, and other relevant parameters under natural, undisturbed conditions. Potential growth can then be estimated for primary or mature secondary forests harvested periodically to maximize wood production. Most growth studies in natural tropical forests (e.g. Veillon and associates, 1983), by contrast, are made in mature or climax forests, which have very low growth rates because photosynthesis serves only to maintain the stand.

The economic accounts consider volume and growth only for species with present market value. These commercial volumes are much lower than the estimates of forest potential, above. In this study, therefore, both economic and physical losses are calculated conservatively.

Results

The deforestation rate in Costa Rica has been extremely high. Deforestation in the tropics as a whole is about 0.5 percent of the existing area annually (WRI, 1988 p. 71), but in Costa Rica the loss has varied between 1.2 percent and 1.8 percent annually from 1970 to 1989, two to three times higher than the inter-national average. From 1966 to 1973, 48.8 thousand ha/yr were deforested, and from 1973 to 1989, 31.8 thousand ha/yr. Over this entire period, Costa Rica lost some 843.9 thousand ha of primary forest, more than 26 percent of the 1963 area. Forests in 1966 covered 58.5 percent of the country. By 1989, however, only an esti-mated 42.9 percent remained in forest.

Most of Costa Rica's deforested land has been turned into pasture (484,635 ha) and annual crops (168,638 ha). Only 35 percent of the total area deforested was converted to agriculture and cattle raising, for which the underlying soils were suited. (See Table A-3.) The rest of the land, 555.7 thousand ha or 65.2 percent of the total area deforested, passed from forest to a use unsuitable for the ecologi-cal and soil conditions.

Table A-3. Deforestation in Costa Rica, by Maximum Land Use Potential, 1966–89 (ha)

Land use capacity[a]	Area deforested	% of total
Annual crops	134,627	15.9%
Permanent and semi-permanent crops	40,436	4.8%
Pasture	119,646	14.1%
Tree crops (plantations)	75,776	8.9%
Forest management	237,822	28.0%
Protection	237,233	28.0%
Undefined	1,863	0.2%
Total	847,403	100.0%

a. Maximum land use potential is the most intensive use sustainable on a site, using traditional management practices. Based on TSC 1985.

The life zones with the highest levels of deforestation are the premontane wet forest and the tropical wet forests, with losses of 285.8 and 212.9 thousand ha, respectively. (See Table A-4.) They are also the life zones in which biodiversity levels are highest. Large losses have also occurred in the wet and moist premontane forests, which are also high in bio-diversity. Deforestation in Costa Rica has thus very likely led to species extinctions—the loss of potential that will never be realized.

Economic Accounts

The concept of economic rent is central to natural resource valuation. *Economic rent* is defined as the return on a production input beyond the minimum required to keep it in its present use (Repetto and associates 1989, p. 19). In forestry economics, *rent* (or profit) is the

Table A-4. Deforestation by Life Zone 1966–89 (ha)

Life Zone[a]	Original Forest Area (1966)	Area Deforested	% of Forest Deforested
Tropical dry forest	55,174	24,445	44.3%
Tropical moist forest	445,841	162,628	36.5%
Tropical wet forest	752,336	212,945	28.3%
Premontane moist forest	280,698	76,070	27.1%
Premontane wet forest	658,527	285,785	43.4%
Premontane rain forest	359,211	69,811	19.4%
Lower montane moist forest	4,546	981	21.6%
Lower montane wet forest	59,458	9,950	16.7%
Lower montane rain forest	304,529	2,555	0.8%
Montane wet forest	327	(349)	b
Montane rain forest	76,055	721	0.9%
Subalpine rain paramo	1,092	(1)	b
Undefined	6,330	1,863	29.4%
Total	3,004,125	847,404	28.2%

a. L.R. Holdridge, *Life Zone Ecology* (San José, Costa Rica: Tropical Science Center) 1967.
b. Apparent regrowth is attributable to map inconsistencies.

difference between income from sales and the cost of forest management and use.

Present Value of Marketable Timber

The wood in a tree is a raw material. It is valuable if it can be transformed into products that can be sold for a profit. This value is known as the *stumpage value* (SV), the difference between the final product market price and the costs of felling, extracting, transporting, and milling a log, including a normal profit margin for each of these intermediate processes.

The economic depreciation due to the loss of a natural resource is equal to the present value of all the benefits provided by that resource. Under perfect market conditions, this value is equal to the price that would have been paid for the resource. For timber in a forest, the stumpage value approximates economic depreciation. Under perfect market conditions, these values are exactly equal.[13]

The natural forest is capable of producing salable products indefinitely. Harvests don't have to draw down forest capital; ideally, only its annual growth should be harvested. On lands best suited to continuing forestry use, the stream of benefits would exceed that generated by agricultural or other uses. Most of the deforested land in Costa Rica has been unsuitable for alternative uses. Consequently, the total value of forest assets is best represented by the discounted net benefits obtained by managing the forest sustainably.

In each hectare of tropical forest live trees of all ages, species, and sizes. Harvesting only mature trees leaves space for the immature trees to grow. Irregular forests are usually best exploited by harvesting only trees over a certain diameter, leaving the best of the rest as growth capital. This capital increases in volume at an annual rate (the mean annual increment), that depends on the site and the type of forest. Forest management generally involves reducing competition from other trees, lianas, and epiphytes to give more valuable species room to grow.

Figure A-2 demonstrates the management of a natural forest. Starting with a previously unharvested forest, all trees larger than 50 cm in diameter would be cut in a harvest year, extracting those with commercial value. In the process, some damage is inevitably done to the residual forest. Harvesting would be followed by forestry operations to increase the growth of the residual forest during a cutting cycle (cc), whose length *equals* the ratio of the extracted volume *plus* damages to the mean annual increment. During this interval, the forest regains its original volume and can once again be harvested. This pattern can be repeated indefinitely. *(See Annex A-4.)*

To determine stumpage values in Costa Rica, three classes of wood were considered: hard, medium, and soft. In Costa Rica, 87 percent of the volume produced is sawn wood for the national market, so domestic prices of sawn wood were used to calculate stumpage values.[14]

The prices in Table A-5 are average prices of sawn wood in the Central Valley, based on 17 representative species (4 hard, 9 medium, and 4 soft) that had price quotations during the entire period. Estimates of prices in non-census years were interpolated using the wood products

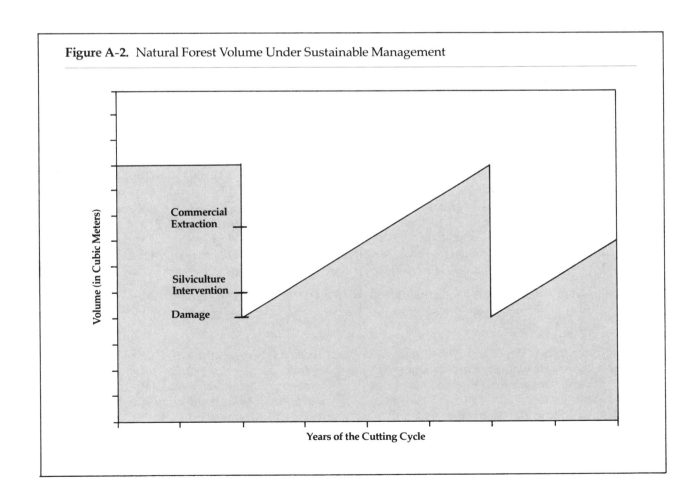

Figure A-2. Natural Forest Volume Under Sustainable Management

Table A-5. Prices of Sawn Wood in Central Valley of Costa Rica (current colones)

Year	Prices of Sawn Wood (colones/m³ of product)			Prices of Sawn Wood (colones/m³ RWE)[a]		
	Hard	Medium	Soft	Hard	Medium	Soft
1970	458	458	265	286	286	166
1971	521	521	302	326	326	189
1972	512	512	297	320	320	186
1973	595	595	345	372	372	215
1974	851	851	493	532	532	308
1975	988	988	572	617	617	358
1976	1,025	1,025	594	641	641	371
1977	1,110	1,110	643	694	694	402
1978	1,209	1,209	700	756	756	438
1979	1,512	1,512	876	945	945	547
1980	1,835	1,835	1,063	1,147	1,147	664
1981	2,455	2,455	1,422	1,534	1,534	889
1982	4,398	4,398	2,547	2,749	2,749	1,592
1983	7,586	7,586	4,394	4,741	4,741	2,746
1984	8,627	8,627	4,997	5,392	5,392	3,123
1985	9,722	9,242	5,280	6,076	5,776	3,300
1986	11,086	9,620	5,368	6,929	6,012	3,355
1987	13,408	10,947	5,998	8,380	6,842	3,749
1988	24,805	17,415	8,111	15,503	10,884	5,069
1989	28,785	20,209	9,412	17,991	12,631	5,883

Sources: Calculated from the Dirección General Forestal, *Censo de la industría forestal,* Departamento de Desarrollo Industrial, San José, Costa Rica, 1975, 1980, 1986, 1987 and 1988; Rodrigo González-Moza, ''Censo de Aserraderos realizado durante enero y febrero 1975,'' Technical Report No. 5, Ministerio de Agricultura y Ganadería, Dirección General Forestal, Departamento Investigación Forestal, San José, Costa Rica, 1976. L. A. Moreira, and E. Palma A., *Boletín Estadístico,* no. 2, Dirección General Forestal, Departamento de Planificación, San José, Costa Rica, 1987; and R.H. Chacón, and O. Gamboa J, *Boletín Estadístico,* no. 3, Dirección General Forestal, Departamento de Planificación, San José, Costa Rica, 1989.

a. 1 m³ of round wood (RWE) is converted to an average of 0.625m³ of sawn wood.

wholesale price index. Prices for 1988 and 1989 were based on round wood prices, assuming that 1987 processing margins remained constant.

Unit costs of extraction, transport, and milling (ET&M) were taken from a detailed feasibility study (DGF, 1984). Costs were classified into six categories and extrapolated from the base year (1984) to the rest of the period, using corresponding price indices. The model also permits total costs to vary with wood type and distance to the sawmill (assuming that the wood is processed in the closest mill). The costs of ET&M are assumed to be 22 percent higher for hard woods than those for medium woods, and soft wood values are assumed to be 60 percent of medium wood values (H. Greub, pers. com., 1990).

The estimate of a normal profit margin is arbitrary but important in the final analysis. If the margin is high, most of the revenue is attributed to the ET&M process, and the calculated stumpage value is low. Nevertheless, the estimated margin should not be below the rate of return on conservative investments during the period. If it were, businesses would have had no reason to invest in timber enterprises. Therefore, the profit margin on harvesting and processing has been estimated at 6 percent, in real terms.

The distance by road from each forest to the nearest sawmill in either San José, Ciudad Quesada, or San Isidro was estimated for all land units that lost more than 3,000 ha of forests during the period: for other areas, that distance was estimated as an average for each cartographic region (nine regions make up the national 1:200,000 map). Next, a weighted average distance from forest to market was calculated for each land unit and the distances were grouped in units of 25 kilometers.

All costs are expressed in colones per cubic meter or round wood equivalents. A summary of the ET&M costs for medium density wood in 1984 at 125 km from a sawmill is shown in Table A-6. Production costs for other years were extrapolated from 1984 data, using the minimum wage index, wholesale prices indices, electricity rates, and exchange rate (¢/US$). *(See Annex A-3.)* Table A-7 presents costs for medium density wood at the same distance for the entire period from 1970 to 1989.

The prices and costs presented are in terms of the value per m³ of round wood, but not every m³ of standing timber reaches the sawmill. In the Sarapiquí study, it was estimated that 1.71 m³ of tree volume is cut for each m³ of roundwood actually extracted from the forest (DGF, 1984a, p. 188). This factor, representing waste and damage, is incorporated into the estimates of stumpage value per m³ of forest volume.

Table A-6. Breakdown of Production Costs of Sawn Wood at 125 Km from Sawmill (1984 values in current colones/m³ of RWE)

	Fuel	Imported equipment	Depreciation of Investment	Labor	Machinery	Insurance	Electricity	Total	%
Normal return on capital[a]	—	—	—	—	—	—	—	370.8	11.8%
Administration	0.5	—	20.2	145.7	32.4	0.6	—	199.4	6.4%
Roads	—	—	28.0	—	123.4	—	—	151.5	4.8%
Preparation	—	—	0.3	44.5	1.9	—	—	46.7	1.5%
Felling and debranching	10.7	7.3	—	41.3	25.5	0.2	—	85.0	2.7%
Extraction	17.9	—	37.9	17.9	40.0	5.2	—	118.9	3.8%
Loading	4.1	—	11.1	10.5	9.2	1.6	—	36.5	1.2%
Transport	101.0	141.2	199.0	66.3	270.2	22.5	—	800.2	25.6%
Milling	44.2	—	309.7	706.3	185.8	—	75.3	1,321.4	42.2%

— Not applicable.

a. The normal return on capital was calculated as 6 percent of the total investment, including one year's working capital.

Table A-7. Costs of Medium Timber Extraction, Transport, and Milling (ET&M) at 125 Km from Sawmill (current colones per m³ RWE)

Year	Costs of Extraction & Transport	Total Costs of ET&M	Year	Costs of Extraction & Transport	Total Costs of ET&M
1970	101.7	233.0	1980	366.1	769.6
1971	107.4	246.8	1981	608.4	1,173.0
1972	111.4	255.4	1982	1,133.1	2,167.0
1973	123.7	281.0	1983	1,420.8	2,834.0
1974	165.0	360.0	1984	1,549.2	3,130.4
1975	194.1	421.2	1985	1,732.2	3,543.6
1976	210.1	460.3	1986	1,901.7	3,915.7
1977	224.9	496.2	1987	2,102.5	4,341.1
1978	242.5	538.5	1988	2,454.9	5,054.1
1979	277.5	608.2	1989	2,802.9	5,841.5

Stumpage values are calculated by subtracting the unit costs of production from the final product price.[15] (See Table A-8 and Figure A-3.)

Rising prices in the late 1980s markedly raised stumpage values. In contrast, throughout much of the 1970s, the stumpage value of soft and hard wood oscillated around zero at a distance of 100 km. Transport costs markedly influence stumpage values. At short distances, exploitation of almost all classes of timber has always been profitable, but only recently have higher prices allowed exploitation of timber at longer distances from sawmills. Figure A-3 compares stumpage values of medium density wood at three different transport distances.[16]

The volumes included in the physical accounts cover the multitude of tree species in different forest types. However, not all species are commercially marketable even today, let alone in past years. Consequently, volume esti-

Table A-8. Stumpage Value of Timber at 125 Km from Sawmill (1984 colones/m³ of RWE)

Year	Hard	Medium	Soft	Year	Hard	Medium	Soft
1970	42	1,008	273	1980	972	1,764	767
1971	438	1,401	502	1981	292	1,023	357
1972	147	1,092	328	1982	143	791	249
1973	420	1,313	473	1983	1,382	2,053	973
1974	955	1,774	764	1984	1,573	2,261	1,088
1975	880	1,668	713	1985	2,146	2,241	986
1976	615	1,403	559	1986	3,004	3,284	2,376
1977	641	1,431	575	1987	2,317	1,879	697
1978	661	1,457	588	1988	5,952	3,716	1,137
1979	1,173	1,947	879	1989	6,044	3,777	1,160

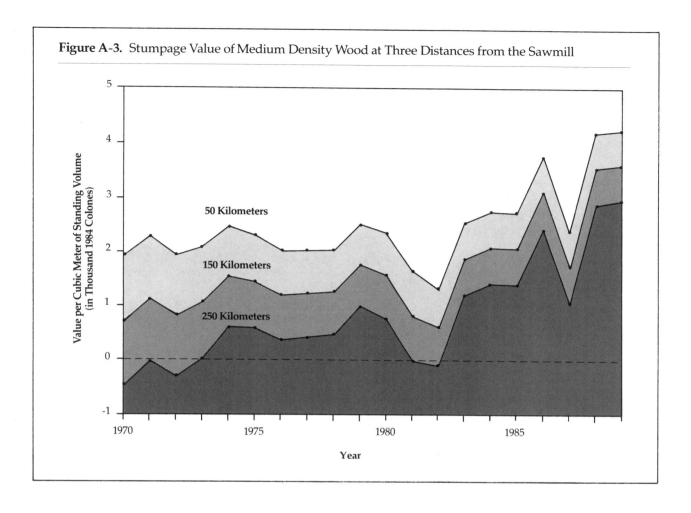

Figure A-3. Stumpage Value of Medium Density Wood at Three Distances from the Sawmill

Value per Cubic Meter of Standing Volume (in Thousand 1984 Colones)

50 Kilometers

150 Kilometers

250 Kilometers

Year

mates must be adjusted to reflect the annual marketable percentage of all species. Only currently marketable species are included in the value accounts; no other species are considered to have stumpage value.

The percentage of marketable wood was estimated from the Sarapiquí study (DGF, 1984), which contains a complete list of marketable and non-marketable tree species. Price lists from industrial censuses were used to identify all species in each density class that had commercial value in at least one place in Costa Rica in 1974, 1984, 1987, or 1988. Finally, percentages were calculated for priced portions of total forest volume in Sarapiquí in each of these years. Through extrapolation and interpolation,

estimates were obtained for the annual marketable fraction of the total volume in each density class from 1970 to 1989. These percentages were applied throughout the country, on the assumption that the Sarapiquí forest is representative of the rest of the nation's forests. Over time, the data show, the percentage of species with market value has increased. *(See Figure A-4.)*

To make the physical and economic accounts consistent, two adjustments were made. First, the value of timber in steeply sloping or inaccessible areas useful only for ecological protection according to the Tropical Science Center land-use classification system (TSC, 1985) was excluded from the economic accounts. Omitting

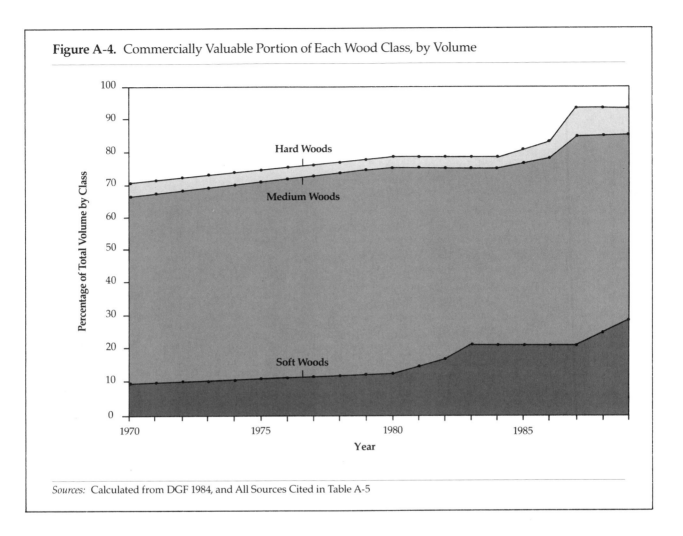

Figure A-4. Commercially Valuable Portion of Each Wood Class, by Volume

Hard Woods

Medium Woods

Soft Woods

Sources: Calculated from DGF 1984, and All Sources Cited in Table A-5

these areas from the economic accounts under-values the resource, but no reliable methodology could be established for valuing the protection function.

Second, only the timber volume in trees larger than 50 cm in diameter at breast height (1.3 m) was included in the physical and value accounts. This is the smallest trunk size that sawmills have traditionally used, although today trees with much smaller diameters are often milled in Costa Rica. Smaller diameter trees were valued in terms of future yields, as described below.

Sustained Value of Production

To estimate timber values under sustained production, the model described above was applied to each forest class in Table A-8, assuming a 15-year minimum cutting cycle. The value of the harvest from the residual forest was estimated by discounting the relevant stumpage values by the factor $1/[(1 + i)^{cc-1}]$ to indicate that the revenue would not be realized until the end of the cutting cycle.

Losses in felling and extracting trees were estimated at 28 percent of residual volume, based on the study of forests in Surinam by Hendrison (1990). For example, if 200 m³/ha remains in a residual forest after exploitation, damage losses would be 56 m³/ha (28 percent of residual volume). If the forest's growth rate were 10 m³/ha/yr, this damage would prolong the cutting cycle by 5.6 years.

The estimated cost of residual forest management in 1990 is approximately 38,000 colones/ha the first harvest year and 2,500 colones/ha each year thereafter in the cutting cycle. These management costs, extrapolated to the relevant years, subtracted from timber stumpage values and appropriately discounted, yield the capital value of future timber harvests, which are forgone when an area is deforested.

In valuing the residual forest, the percentage of marketable species must also be taken into account. For the residual forest, these percentages will be higher later in the cycle than in the first year because the number of marketable species increases over time. To estimate the percentages of marketable volume in the future, a function was established that allowed for gradual increases in the percentage for each wood class over time.[17]

The total decline in the value of the forest asset due to deforestation, therefore, has two components. The first is the value of the timber marketable in the year in which deforestation takes place. The second is the potential future timber revenues lost when the forest is converted to other uses.

Forest Resource Appreciation

Secondary Forests

Secondary forests grow mostly on abandoned cattle ranches and on farms with depleted soils. The timber volume in a secondary forest depends on site and forest age. The site's forestry potential cannot be regained in a single rotation, because potential growth is reduced by the degradation of the original ecosystem, nutrient loss, and soil compaction during the previous land use. Furthermore, the species diversity is poorer than in the original forest, and most of the valuable species have disappeared.

Thus, poorer grade secondary forests are valuable primarily for firewood, posts, and minor products—not for sawn timber (Herrera, 1990).[18] Most of these products are consumed on the farm or locally, with minimal transport costs. In 1989, the average value of the standing volume of secondary forest was 1,488 current colones/m³ (See Annex A-5). Since these values are derived directly from posts and firewood, the annual increment in the total volume increases the value of the asset proportionately.

From 1963 to 1984, the area under secondary forest declined slightly from 299,000 ha² to 229,000 ha². (See Table A-9), but the average age of these forests increased. Since the early 1980s, the total area in agriculture and cattle raising does not seem to have changed, but as incentives to cattle raising have fallen, more and more degraded pastures have been abandoned. For these reasons, it is assumed that the decline in primary forest area due to deforestation since 1984 has been accompanied by an equal and opposite change in the secondary forest area.[19]

Herrera found that the growth rate in secondary forests in Sarapiquí and Turrialba ranged from 5.4 m³ and 8.4 m³/ha/yr and estimated that these forests could reach up to 12 m³/ha/yr under management. Secondary forests older than 40 years were found to have growth rates of only 2.6 m³/ha/yr. Because most of Costa Rica's secondary forests have only recently been established, a growth rate of 5 m³/ha/yr was assumed for the present study.

These values imply that approximately 1.9 million m³ of wood is being produced annually in the nation's secondary forests. Because most of this resource is not now being used, the volume of timber in secondary forests is appreciating. (See Figure A-5.) By 1989, an estimated 388,000 ha² were under secondary forests, almost 14 times the area in forestry plantations.

Table A-9. Secondary Forest: Area and Volume

Year	Initial Area (ha)	Average Age (yr)	Initial Volume ('000 m³)	Annual Growth ('000 m³)	Area Cut (ha)	Volume Cut ('000 m³)	Area Abandoned (ha)
1963	299,011	5.0	7,475	1,495	29,901	897	28,357
1964	297,467	5.4	8,073	1,487	29,747	956	28,203
1965	295,923	5.8	8,605	1,480	29,592	1,008	28,048
1966	294,379	6.2	9,076	1,472	29,438	1,055	27,894
1967	292,835	6.5	9,493	1,464	29,284	1,096	27,740
1968	291,291	6.8	9,861	1,456	29,129	1,132	27,585
1969	289,747	7.0	10,186	1,449	28,975	1,163	27,431
1970	288,203	7.3	10,471	1,441	28,820	1,191	27,276
1971	286,659	7.5	10,721	1,433	28,666	1,215	27,122
1972	285,115	7.7	10,939	1,426	28,512	1,236	26,968
1973	283,571	7.8	11,128	1,418	28,357	1,255	23,413
1974	278,627	8.1	11,291	1,393	27,863	1,268	22,919
1975	273,683	8.3	11,416	1,368	27,368	1,278	22,425
1976	268,740	8.6	11,506	1,344	26,874	1,285	21,930
1977	263,796	8.8	11,565	1,319	26,380	1,288	21,436
1978	258,852	9.0	11,595	1,294	25,885	1,289	20,941
1979	253,908	9.1	11,601	1,270	25,391	1,287	20,447
1980	248,965	9.3	11,583	1,245	24,896	1,283	19,953
1981	244,021	9.5	11,545	1,220	24,402	1,277	19,458
1982	239,077	9.6	11,489	1,195	23,908	1,268	18,964
1983	234,133	9.8	11,416	1,171	23,413	1,259	18,470
1984	229,189	9.9	11,328	1,146	22,919	1,247	54,749
1985	261,020	8.6	11,226	1,305	26,102	1,253	57,932
1986	292,850	7.7	11,278	1,464	29,285	1,274	61,115
1987	324,680	7.1	11,468	1,623	32,468	1,309	64,298
1988	356,510	6.6	11,782	1,783	35,651	1,357	67,481
1989	388,341	6.3	12,209	1,942	38,834	1,415	70,664

Note: Areas from 1963 and 1973 were taken from the agricultural censuses (Dirección General de Estadística y Censos, 1966 and 1974). The 1984 area was derived from the 1984 land use map (IGN, 1985). Areas in non-census years from 1963 to 1983 were estimated using straight line interpolations, while the areas for 1985 to 1989 were estimated assuming a constant rate of increase equal to the estimated rate of deforestation of primary forest. The secondary forest area cut annually was set at 10 percent of the area existing at the beginning of the year. Abandoned areas were then calculated using a residual sum equation to assure that the resulting final area coincided exactly with the initial area of the following year.

Yet, despite the magnitude of this resource's potential, neither the authorities nor the land owners consider these forests valuable.

The annual change in the value of the secondary forest resource is calculated in Table A-10. In 1989 alone, the value of this asset

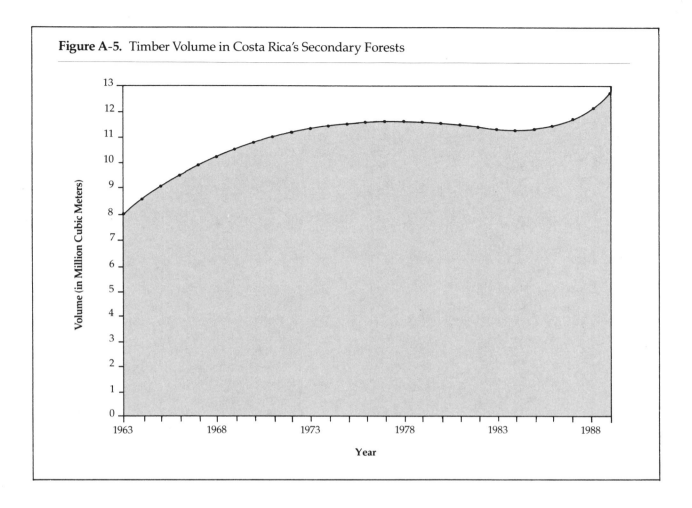

Figure A-5. Timber Volume in Costa Rica's Secondary Forests

Volume (in Million Cubic Meters)

Year

increased US$8 million. Although reforestation projects have received much attention and the benefit of government incentives, the area of secondary forests far exceeds that of plantations, and their value is fast growing. This underexploited resource deserves still more research and other support.

Results: Depreciation of Forest Asset

Costa Rica's forests are an economic asset capable of producing important economic benefits, both directly through marketable products and indirectly through watershed protection, environmental stability, tourism, and other forest-dependent activities. But deforestation

Costa Rica's forests are an economic asset capable of producing important economic benefits, but deforestation represents a fantastic waste of the nation's natural resources.

represents a fantastic waste of the nation's natural resources. The most direct measure of this waste is the volume of commercial wood lost *(see Table A-11)*—enough to have produced 1

27

Table A-10. Economic Value of Costa Rica's Secondary Forests

Year	Total Resource Value (million 1984 ¢)	Change in Volume ('000 m³)	Change in Value (millions)		
			(current colones)	(constant colones)	(1984 US$)
1966	6,406	417	17.5	281.5	6.3
1967	6,655	368	16.0	248.7	5.6
1968	6,874	325	14.7	219.1	4.9
1969	7,066	285	13.5	192.5	4.3
1970	7,235	250	12.6	168.6	3.8
1971	7,382	218	11.9	147.0	3.3
1972	7,509	189	10.7	127.6	2.9
1973	7,620	163	10.0	110.2	2.5
1974	7,704	125	9.6	84.1	1.9
1975	7,765	90	8.3	60.7	1.4
1976	7,804	59	6.2	39.6	0.9
1977	7,825	31	3.6	20.7	0.5
1978	7,828	5	0.7	3.6	0.1
1979	7,817	− 17	− 2.6	− 11.8	− 0.3
1980	7,791	− 38	− 6.8	− 25.6	− 0.6
1981	7,753	− 56	− 12.3	− 38.1	− 0.9
1982	7,704	− 73	− 28.3	− 49.3	− 1.1
1983	7,644	− 88	− 50.6	− 59.4	− 1.3
1984	7,576	− 101	− 68.4	− 68.4	− 1.5
1985	7,611	52	42.3	35.1	0.8
1986	7,739	190	178.7	128.2	2.9
1987	7,951	314	334.7	212.1	4.8
1988	8,239	426	522.5	287.5	6.5
1989	8,594	527	784.2	355.4	8.0

Note: Assumes 1989 value of 1,489 colones/m³. Source: Annex A-5 and Table A-9.

million mt of pulp for paper in 1963 and 640 thousand mt in 1989. The total volume of timber lost annually between 1963 and 1989 ranged from 10.2 million m³ to 15.7 million m³ annually. Of this total, an average of 26.4 percent is estimated to be commercial volume, of which only 43 percent was actually transformed into industrial products. The net utilization rate therefore is only about 11 percent of the total standing volume lost through deforestation.

Although the annual deforestation rate is estimated to have declined sharply since 1973,

the economic loss per hectare deforested has increased rapidly with rising wood prices in recent years. *(See Table A-12.)*

These results reflect various problems already identified in the Costa Rican Tropical Forest Action Plan (MIRINEM, 1990a):

- low rates of utilization of the timber volumes in tropical forests;

- inefficiency within the industry and high tolerance for waste of potentially marketable wood;

Table A-11. Total Volume of Timber Deforested and Portion Used by the Sawmilling Industry (million m³, standing volume)

	Volume Deforested		Volume Processed[b]		
Year	Total	Commercial[a]	Round Wood	Standing Volume	% of Commercial Volume Processed
1970	15.7	3.2	0.9	1.5	45.3%
1971	15.7	3.4	0.9	1.5	42.3%
1972	15.7	3.3	0.8	1.4	42.9%
1973	15.7	3.6	0.8	1.4	39.3%
1974	10.8	2.8	0.8	1.4	49.2%
1975	10.8	2.9	0.8	1.4	47.9%
1976	10.8	2.9	0.8	1.3	46.6%
1977	10.8	2.9	0.8	1.3	45.4%
1978	10.8	3.0	0.8	1.3	44.1%
1979	10.8	3.0	0.8	1.3	42.2%
1980	10.8	3.1	0.7	1.3	41.0%
1981	10.8	2.7	0.7	1.3	45.7%
1982	10.8	2.8	0.7	1.2	45.0%
1983	10.8	3.2	0.7	1.2	39.0%
1984	10.8	3.2	0.7	1.2	39.3%
1985	10.3	2.9	0.7	1.3	42.9%
1986	10.3	3.0	0.7	1.3	42.5%
1987	10.3	3.2	0.8	1.3	40.3%
1988	10.2	3.2	0.8	1.3	42.7%
1989	10.2	3.2	0.8	1.4	43.7%

Sources: Columns 2 and 3, this study; columns 4 and 5, Dirección General Forestal, *Censo de la industría forestal*, Departamento de Desarrollo Industrial, San José, Costa Rica, 1988; L.A. Moreira, and E. Palma A., *Boletín Estadístico*, no. 2, Dirección General Forestal, Departamento de Planificación, San José, Costa Rica, 1987; and Chacón H., and O. Gamboa J, *Boletín Estadístico*, no. 3, Dirección General Forestal, Departamento de Planificación, San José, Costa Rica, 1989.

a. Commercial volume includes timber over 50 cm in diameter with a positive market value and excludes forests suitable only for protection.

b. Volume actually processed estimated from DGF forest industry censuses. It is assumed that 1 m³ of round wood in the patio of a sawmill equals 1.71 m³ of standing volume.

- ignorance of sustainable forestry techniques; and

- ignorance of the many public and private non-timber values of the forest.

The annual depreciation due to deforestation has ranged from 1.8 billion colones (US$42 million) to 18.8 billion colones (US$422 million). In 1984, for example, the total value of the forests lost was $167.3 million—$69 for each man, woman, and child in Costa Rica. In 1988 and 1989, depreciation of the forest asset cost the nation an estimated 36 percent more than payments on its public external debt. Yet the

Table A-12. Economic Value of Primary Forest Deforested (thousand colones/ha)

Year	Total Area Deforested (ha)	Commercial Area Deforested[a] (ha)	Value/ha Deforested ('000 1984 ¢)	Value/Commercial ha Deforested ('000 1984 ¢)
1970	48,827	18,806	65.8	170.8
1971	48,827	27,763	99.2	174.4
1972	48,827	22,658	75.5	162.8
1973	48,827	27,862	95.8	167.9
1974	31,830	22,765	157.9	220.7
1975	31,830	22,765	146.9	205.4
1976	31,830	22,008	117.0	169.2
1977	31,830	22,008	120.7	174.6
1978	31,830	22,008	124.3	179.7
1979	31,830	22,765	185.6	259.5
1980	31,830	22,765	165.1	230.9
1981	31,830	14,411	82.8	182.8
1982	31,830	8,481	59.3	222.7
1983	31,830	22,810	207.7	289.8
1984	31,830	22,833	234.0	326.2
1985	31,830	20,733	242.8	372.7
1986	31,830	20,979	370.7	562.4
1987	31,830	20,697	247.5	380.6
1988	31,830	20,818	571.1	873.2
1989	31,830	20,659	577.5	889.8

a. Excludes forests suitable only for protection and those with no commercial value.

depreciation of the forest asset has gone largely unnoticed by Costa Rica's economic policy-makers. *(See Table A-13.)*

This depreciation has been only partially off-set by appreciation in the value of secondary forests—603 million current colones in 1989. Under management, the asset value of secondary forests could be increased much more. Clearly, these neglected areas warrant far more attention than they are getting.

The destruction of the nation's forests has absorbed more than the forestry sector's entire economic contribution during the study period. The total value added by the forestry and forest industry sectors was less than the annual depreciation of the forest asset in all but two years. *(See Figure A-6.)* Net value added in forestry is consequently negative for the period. Nonetheless, Costa Rica's forest sector could have been an important producer without depreciating its natural resource asset, if it had used a higher percentage of the total wood cut and managed both primary and secondary forests sustainably on those lands suitable for forestry development.

Table A-13. Depreciation of Costa Rica's Forest Resource and the Resulting Net Forestry Product (million 1984 colones)

Year	Depreciation			Appreciation of Secondary Forests	Gross Forestry Product[a]	Net Forestry Product
	Loss of Standing Timber	Loss of Future Harvests	Total			
1970	2,997	214	3,211	(169)	—	—
1971	4,195	648	4,843	(147)	—	—
1972	3,279	409	3,688	(128)	—	—
1973	4,003	676	4,679	(110)	—	—
1974	4,091	934	5,025	(84)	—	—
1975	3,871	804	4,675	(61)	—	—
1976	3,212	512	3,724	(40)	—	—
1977	3,313	531	3,844	(21)	—	—
1978	3,407	548	3,955	(4)	2,829	−1,123
1979	4,835	1,074	5,909	12	3,059	−2,861
1980	4,356	901	5,257	26	3,024	−2,258
1981	2,430	205	2,635	38	3,029	357
1982	1,854	35	1,889	49	2,189	251
1983	5,395	1,215	6,610	59	2,527	−4,143
1984	6,010	1,439	7,449	68	3,071	−4,446
1985	6,193	1,535	7,728	(35)	2,917	−4,776
1986	9,224	2,575	11,799	(128)	2,968	−8,703
1987	6,463	1,414	7,877	(212)	2,746	−4,920
1988	14,175	4,003	18,178	(288)	—	—
1989	14,326	4,057	18,383	(355)	—	—

— Not available.
a. Calculated from Table A-1.

31

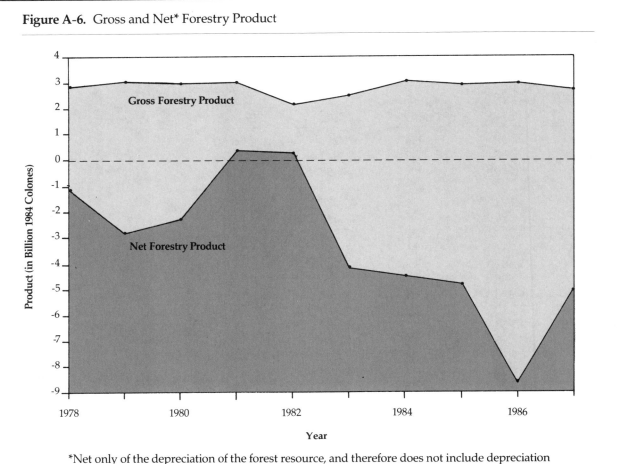

Figure A-6. Gross and Net* Forestry Product

Product (in Billion 1984 Colones)

Gross Forestry Product

Net Forestry Product

1978 1980 1982 1984 1986

Year

*Net only of the depreciation of the forest resource, and therefore does not include depreciation of man-made capital.

B. Soil Accounts

Costa Rica's wide range of natural resources has facilitated crop production (coffee, bananas, cocoa, and sugar cane) and cattle ranching. In 1984, agriculture generated around 30 percent of the gross national product, 33 percent of national employment, and 54.5 percent of foreign exchange. The interconnections between the national economy and soil quality are close and important.

Land-use patterns have shifted dramatically since the 1950's as large parts of the nation's vast forests have been cleared for pastures. *(See Table B-1.)* Much of this recently cleared land is too poor for profitable farming. *(See Table A-3).*

The misuse of land has decreased its productive capacity. Hartshorn and associates (1982, pp. 82–85) estimated that light to moderate erosion has depleted a quarter of Costa Rica's soil and that another fifth has been severely eroded.

Cattle ranching is the chief source of land misuse. Even in good times, the land can sus-

Table B-1. Agricultural Land Use, Costa Rica 1950–84 (thousand ha)

Use	Years				
	1950[a]	1955[a]	1963[b]	1973[b]	1984[c]
Annual crops	111.7	114.8	409.3	283.3	412.8
Perennial crops	99.2	124.8	200.3	207.1	252.2
Pasture	625.1	907.3	935.2	1,558.0	1,770.2
Total	836.0	1,146.9	1,544.8	2,048.4	2,435.2

a. MIRINEM, Ministerio de Recursos Naturales, Energía y Minas, *Plan de Acción Forestal de Costa Rica, Documento Base*, San José, Costa Rica, 1990.

b. Dirección General de Estadística y Censos, *Censo Agropecuario—1973* and *Censo Agropecuario—1963*, Ministerio de Industria y Comercio, San José, Costa Rica, 1966 and 1974.

c. Results from this study based upon: Dirección General de Estadística y Censos, *Censo Agropecuario—1984*, Ministerio de Industria y Comercio, San José, Costa Rica, 1985...; and IGN 1984.

tain on average only 0.9 head of cattle per hectare nationally. (SEPSA Secretaria de Planificación Sectorial Agropecuaria 1990). As economic decline has hit ranching over the last decade, large tracts of spoiled pastures have been abandoned. In other areas, where erosion of steep, clean-tilled surfaces has cut the land's productivity, pastures have replaced crops. The district of Puriscal, for example, was once an important producer of corn and beans. After erosion cut productivity, the land was converted to grazing.

Depreciation of the Soil Resource

A soil's fertility depends on its slope, texture, depth, and structure as well as on precipitation, temperature, and other ecological conditions. As long as soil use does not exceed its capacity, productivity can be maintained indefinitely. If overused, the soil's productivity wanes, economic value is lost, and eventually the land is abandoned.

If managed poorly the soil gradually loses productivity. Inputs have to be intensified to maintain the same yield, or farmers are forced to switch to less intensive and profitable crops.[20] These problems all result from nutrient loss and the deterioration of soil structure.

The depreciation of the soil resource can be expressed directly, by quantifying the loss of productivity, or indirectly, by evaluating physical and biological properties lost through erosion and leaching.

Depreciation: Productivity Measure

Erosion results from wind, rain, and other factors beyond man's control and from controllable factors such as cultivation methods. Although exactly how much soil any piece of land will lose cannot be predicted, once erosion begins, it continues until land use or soil-management practices improve. With every year of misuse, nutrients wash away, physical characteristics deteriorate, and productive capacity drops.

Like any asset, the value of the soil *equals* the present value of its future potential earning. Real depreciation occurs whenever a decline in productivity reduces this value. Because productivity loss is permanent unless resource management improves, one year's soil loss causes economic losses at each successive harvest. Assuming constant prices, the present value of the loss can be expressed as:

(1) $VSD = (Rp_R - Cp_c)/i$,
where:

VSD = value of soil resource depreciation
R = original soil income
p_R = proportional loss of income through erosion
C = operating costs
p_c = proportional change in operating costs and
i = interest rate.[21]

Quantification of productivity loss is information-intensive. Data are needed on:

• physical and biological soil loss

• the relationship between soil loss and normal crop productivity in the type of soil analyzed[22]

• crop economics, including labor, input, and machinery requirements and costs, harvest volumes, and product prices.

The relationship between erosion and soil productivity can change over time. Use of new technology and inputs may improve productivity, despite erosion. Magrath and Arens (1989) demonstrated that such productivity increases may mask real losses from reduced potential as a result of erosion.

Depreciation: Replacement Cost Method

Nutrient content is one of the most important soil characteristics for crop growth. Erosion translates physically into the depth of soil washed away, varying in severity from a few millimeters to several centimeters. With the soil go nutrients, principally nitrogen (N), phosphorous (P), and potassium (K). To restore soil fertility, nutrients would have to be replaced through fertilization (Yost and associates, 1985 pp. 248–61).

Depreciation can, therefore, be estimated as the cost of replacing lost nutrients with commercial fertilizers:[23]

(2) $VSD = (QN_{tot} - QN_{tol}) \cdot (f_a)(P_f + C_f)$,
where:

QN_{tot} = total quantity of nutrients lost
QN_{tol} = tolerable quantity of loss
f_a = factor to account for fertilizer efficiency
P_f = price of fertilizers, and
C_f = cost of applying one unit of fertilizer.

The methodology, though simple, has a few limitations:

• Nutrients are usually concentrated in the upper layers of soil. For example, more nutrients are lost from the first centimeter than from the twentieth. In national level analysis, each unit of soil volume must be assumed equal in nutrients, since the depth to which loss occurs is unknown.

• Soil cannot lose value indefinitely. Once erosion and nutrient loss become severe, soil can no longer support most crops (Gregersen and associates, 1988, p. 45). This point cannot be determined if the extent of productive capacity loss is unknown.

• Soil has some recuperative capacity because it is formed by deterioration of organic material from above and geological decay from below. Some erosion and depth loss can therefore be sustained without productivity losses (Bennett, 1939; Lombardi and Bertoni, 1975). To allow for this recuperative capacity, net erosion loss is taken as equivalent to the difference between the total and tolerable soil erosion. Estimation of the tolerable level of soil erosion is, however, difficult and imprecise.

The replacement cost method is never exact. It undervalues true depreciation for profitable crops and overvalues it for less profitable crops. The productivity loss method is theoretically much more precise. Correctly used, this method reflects the true relationship between soil loss and real economic loss, linking diminished to decreased productivity.

Both models are seriously limited by lack of measured data on soil loss. Ideally, measurements would be made on experimental runoff plots under a variety of ground covers and ecological conditions. In Costa Rica, however, the few experimental erosion plots are too new to provide useful information.

Soil loss can be estimated with models that combine the effects of several key variables. Designed originally for temperate climates and agricultural practices, these must be adjusted for site-specific conditions in the tropics. The model most often used is the universal soil loss equation or USLE (Wischmeier and Smith, 1978).

The USLE has been used in many countries, including Costa Rica. Vásquez (1989) used this formula to estimate erosion throughout the country. Based on preliminary studies carried out in a few areas such as Puriscal (CORENA/MAG 1984) and on the Country Environmental Profile (Hartshorn and associates, 1982), this study's results appear to underestimate true erosion. Tosi (1980, pp. 34–39) also utilized the USLE equation to estimate erosion for the Arenal Basin.

Many attempts have been made to correlate erosion with productivity loss. The lack of data in most developing countries, however, makes most models difficult to apply, especially at the national level.

- Pierce and associates (1983) proposed a model called the erosion and productivity index calculator (EPIC), using mathematical simulation to assess relative potential soil productivity.

- Larson and associates (1985) based their productivity index (PI) method upon the variation of non-substitutable soil attributes that depend on subsoil properties.

- Onstad and Young (1988) subdivided the land into cells, calculated productivity indexes for each of them, then analyzed the effects of erosion, based on erosion-productivity models. This method also demands abundant edaphic and agronomic statistics about the study area.

- Magrath and Arens (1989) assessed the economic impact of erosion in Indonesia, estimating the reduction in yields in various crops on different land classes. The results of this study are specific to the island of Java and cannot be extrapolated to other countries.

- Biot (1988) used productivity indices relating the soil's loss of capacity to retain moisture directly to erosion. The method seems reasonable, but the model would have to be recalibrated for use in Costa Rica.

In summary, neither the replacement cost method nor productivity loss models is ideal for Costa Rica. The productivity loss models, though conceptually superior, require agronomic studies to develop a workable data base. For this reason, the replacement cost method was chosen for erosion analysis at the national level. (For a preliminary analysis of depreciation in terms of productivity using the EPIC model, *see* Annex B-1.)

Valuation of Costa Rica's Soil Loss

Methodology: Physical Accounts

The universal soil loss equation (Wischmeier and Smith, 1978) is a parametric model for evaluating sheet and rill erosion, using the equation:

(3) $\quad A = R \cdot K \cdot L \cdot S \cdot C \cdot P,$
where:

$\quad A$ = soil loss per unit of surface area
$\quad R$ = rainfall and runoff factor
$\quad K$ = soil erosiveness factor
$\quad L$ = slope length factor

S = slope grade factor
C = crop cover affectivity parameter, and
P = the soil conservation practices factor.

Data Utilized. The values of K, L, and S used in this study were derived from a map developed in a Costa Rican soil-use study at 1:200,000 (Vásquez, 1989). The soil erosivity factor, K, varies by soil class and is highly dependent on soil texture and clay mineral content. The slope and length factors, S and L, are derived from slope and relief parameters measured in the national topographic map. These characteristics were grouped into 22 classes of soil types (Annex B-2), according to their erosion potential. *(See Table B-2.)* The R factor was obtained from Vahrson (1989). The C factor depends upon actual land use, which was determined for each year during the period using maps for 1966 (IGN, 1970) and 1984 (IGN, 1985) and agricultural census data from 1963, 1973 and 1984.[24] Finally, considering general absence of soil conservation practices in Costa Rica, the soil management factor, P, was assumed to have a value of 1.0.

Table B-3 presents the range of erosion rates, estimated with an R factor of 425 for a zone of moderate rain erosivity. Estimated erosion rates range from virtually nil to a maximum of 647 mt/ha/yr.

Tolerable erosion rates must be subtracted from total erosion to estimate soil depreciation. To estimate tolerable erosion (A_{tol}), the management practices needed to sustain each type of soil use were first estimated.[25] Then, following López and associates (1987), the numeric value of factors C and P for each sustainable use were obtained. The combination of C • P with the greatest product was identified as the maximum sustainable use of the soil.[26]

Applying the maximum sustainable C • P factor to each soil class in each of the nine different values of R, the maximum sustainable level of erosion was obtained in tons per hectare per year. *(See Table B-4.)* The non-sustainable or non-tolerable erosion rate for a particular soil in a particular place, therefore, was derived from the total erosion loss *less* the

Table B-2. Erosion Potential by Soil Type, Costa Rica

Soil Type[a]	L&S Factor	K Factor	Soil Type[a]	L&S Factor	K Factor
A-1	0.35	0.28	F-1	8.71	0.20
A-2	0.35	0.19	F-2-1	0.35	0.30
A-3	0.35	0.08	F-2-2	0.35	0.18
B-1	0.35	0.26	F-2-3	3.86	0.35
B-2	0.35	0.36	F-2-4	3.86	0.20
C-1	2.11	0.25	F-2-5	11.79	0.29
C-2	2.11	0.18	F-2-6	11.79	0.38
D-1	5.62	0.24	G-1	15.00	0.20
D-2	5.62	0.16	G-2	15.00	0.25
E-1	11.79	0.12	G-3	15.00	0.22
E-2	11.79	0.12	G-4	15.00	0.25

Note: USLE length, slope, and soil erodibility values (L, S, and K factors) for each slope type in Costa Rica.

a. See Annex B-2 for description of soil types.

Table B-3. Total Erosion by Soil Type and Use (mt/ha/yr)

Soil Type	K•L•S Factor	Forest	Pasture	Perennial Crops	Annual Crops
				USLE C-Factor	
		0.003	0.04	0.86	0.34
A-1	0.10	0.1	1.6	3.6	14.2
A-2	0.07	0.1	1.2	2.4	9.6
A-3	0.03	0.0	0.4	1.0	4.0
B-1	0.09	0.1	1.6	3.3	13.1
B-2	0.13	0.2	2.0	4.6	18.2
C-1	0.53	0.7	8.8	19.3	76.2
C-2	0.38	0.5	6.4	13.9	54.9
D-1	1.35	1.7	22.8	49.3	194.9
D-2	0.90	1.1	15.2	32.9	129.9
E-1	1.41	1.8	24.0	51.7	204.4
E-2	1.41	1.8	24.0	51.7	204.4
F-1	1.74	2.2	29.6	63.7	251.7
F-2-1	0.11	0.1	1.6	3.8	15.2
F-2-2	0.06	0.1	1.2	2.3	9.1
F-2-3	1.35	1.7	22.8	49.4	195.2
F-2-4	0.77	1.0	13.2	28.2	111.6
F-2-5	3.42	4.4	58.0	125.0	494.1
F-2-6	4.48	5.7	76.0	163.8	647.4
G-1	3.00	3.8	51.2	109.7	433.5
G-2	3.75	4.8	63.6	137.1	541.9
G-3	3.30	4.2	56.0	120.6	476.9
G-4	3.75	4.8	63.6	137.1	541.9

Note: Assumes an *R* factor of 425.

climate-specific tolerable erosion levels presented in Table B-4.

The net erosion per hectare was then converted into quantities of the most important available nutrients (nitrogen N, phosphorous P, and potassium K). *(See Table B-5.)* Nutrient content estimates for each type of soil were based on data from Bertsch (1987) and unpublished data from SENACSA (Servicio Nacional de Conservación de Suelos y Agua). The methodology presented here follows Cruz and associates (1988) with some modifications for Costa Rican conditions. (For a technical discussion of the N, P, and K levels used here, *see* Annex B-3.)

Only a little of the available nitrogen mineralizes each year—5 percent for most soils, 2 percent for volcanic soils.[27] For this study, it was conservatively assumed that nitrogen could be restored after two years of good soil management. The nitrogen loss per ton of soil eroded is assumed to be twice the nitrogen mineralized annually. Finally, nutrient losses were converted to commercial fertilizer equivalents using the values presented in Table B-6.[28]

The following conservative assumptions were made about the value of lost nutrients during this study.

Table B-4. Tolerable Erosion, by Soil and Climate (mt/ha/yr)

Soil Type	P Max[a]	C Max[a,b]	R Factor 85	155	255	425	595	765	935	1105	1275	1445
A-1	0.60	AC	1.7	3.1	5.1	8.5	11.9	15.3	18.7	22.1	25.5	28.9
A-2	0.60	AC	1.2	2.1	3.5	5.8	8.1	10.4	12.7	15.0	17.3	19.6
A-3	0.60	AC	0.5	0.9	1.5	2.4	3.4	4.4	5.3	6.3	7.3	8.3
B-1	0.60	AC	1.6	2.9	4.7	7.9	11.0	14.2	17.4	20.5	23.7	26.8
B-2	0.60	AC	2.2	4.0	6.6	10.9	15.3	19.7	24.0	28.4	32.8	37.1
C-1	0.10	AC	1.5	2.8	4.6	7.6	10.7	13.7	16.8	19.8	22.9	25.9
C-2	0.10	AC	1.1	2.0	3.3	5.5	7.7	9.9	12.1	14.3	16.5	18.7
D-1	0.80	PA	3.7	6.7	11.0	18.3	25.7	33.0	40.4	47.7	55.0	62.4
D-2	0.80	PA	2.4	4.5	7.3	12.2	17.1	22.0	26.9	31.8	36.7	41.6
E-1	0.06	PC	0.6	1.1	1.9	3.1	4.3	5.6	6.8	8.1	9.3	10.5
E-2	0.06	PC	0.6	1.1	1.9	3.1	4.3	5.6	6.8	8.1	9.3	10.5
F-1	0.06	PC	0.8	1.4	2.3	3.8	5.3	6.9	8.4	9.9	11.5	13.0
F-2-1	0.60	AC	1.8	3.3	5.5	9.1	12.7	16.4	20.0	23.7	27.3	31.0
F-2-2	0.60	AC	1.1	2.0	3.3	5.5	7.6	9.8	12.0	14.2	16.4	18.6
F-2-3	0.14	AC	5.5	10.0	16.4	27.3	38.3	49.2	60.1	71.1	82.0	92.9
F-2-4	0.14	AC	3.1	5.7	9.4	15.6	21.9	28.1	34.4	40.6	46.9	53.1
F-2-5	0.90	PA	10.5	19.1	31.4	52.3	73.2	94.2	115.1	136.0	156.9	177.9
F-2-6	0.90	PA	13.7	25.0	41.1	68.5	96.0	123.4	150.8	178.2	205.6	233.1
G-1	1.00	FO	0.8	1.4	2.3	3.8	5.4	6.9	8.4	9.9	11.5	13.0
G-2	1.00	FO	1.0	1.7	2.9	4.8	6.7	8.6	10.5	12.4	14.3	16.3
G-3	1.00	FO	0.8	1.5	2.5	4.2	5.9	7.6	9.3	10.9	12.6	14.3
G-4	1.00	FO	1.0	1.7	2.9	4.8	6.7	8.6	10.5	12.4	14.3	16.3

a. *C* and *P* maximum describe in numeric form the sustainable use that would produce the most erosion.

b. The use codes refer to the following uses and C-factor values: AC = annual crops, 0.34; PC = perennial crops, 0.86; PA = pasture, 0.04; FO = forest, 0.003.

- It was assumed that all nutrient losses from erosion can be replaced by the use of fertilizers which is not always the case.

- Only losses of nitrogen, phosphorous, and potassium are considered. These losses do not include other lost elements such as calcium, magnesium, sulfur, and oligoelements, which may equal the loss of potassium (for calcium and magnesium) and phosphorous (for sulfur). The physical deterioration of the soil—difficult to quantify but essential to productivity management—is not measured either.

- It is assumed that erosion in forest areas is sustainable, so nutrient loss in these areas is ignored.

- All types of land use are subsumed into only 4 categories, and soils into 22 classes.

Each value is therefore an average and not necessarily accurate for a particular site. The study results are thus limited by the scale of the work. Likewise, the *R* factor was calculated with a map at a scale of 1:1,000,000, which further limits the precision of the results.

Table B-5. Available Nutrients by Soil Type (g/mt)

Soil Type	Nitrogen	Phosphorus	Potassium	Soil Type	Nitrogen	Phosphorus	Potassium
A-1	195.0	15	9.75	F-1	175.5	10	1.95
A-2	156.0	10	7.80	F-2-1	117.0	10	1.56
A-3	117.0	10	3.12	F-2-2	117.0	10	1.56
B-1	390.0	20	2.34	F-2-3	234.0	15	2.34
B-2	292.5	12	1.56	F-2-4	140.4	5	1.95
C-1	234.0	2	1.95	F-2-5	117.0	5	1.95
C-2	292.5	2	1.56	F-2-6	175.5	5	1.95
D-1	156.0	10	1.56	G-1	312.0	10	1.17
D-2	234.0	10	1.56	G-2	292.5	10	1.17
E-1	156.0	6	1.56	G-3	46.8	30	3.90
E-2	312.0	5	0.78	G-4	234.0	5	1.56

Note: The characteristics of the soil classes are presented in Annex B-2.

Sources: The N, P, and K contents for most soils were obtained from F. Bertsch, Manual Para Interpretar la Fertilidad de los Suelos de Costa Rica, 2d ed. (San José, Costa Rica: Escuela de Fitotecnica, Universidad de Costa Rica), 1987. Data for mountainous soils, came from Servicio Nacional de Conservación de Suelos y Agua.

Table B-6. Conversion Values, Nutrient Losses to Commercial Fertilizers

Element	Fertilizer	Percent of Pure Nutrient	Fertilizer Efficiency Rate	Kg of Fertilizer per Kg of Element Lost
N	Urea	46%	50%	4.35
K	Potassium muriate	52%	80%	2.40
P	Triple super-phosphate	46%	25%	8.70

Source: Elemer Bornemisza, pers. com. (1990).

Methodology: Economic Accounts

Once the volume of eroded soil was determined and expressed in fertilizer terms, the price farmers would pay for replacement fertilizers was determined. *(See Table B-7.)* Fertilizer transport costs were excluded because they would have yielded the counterintuitive result that erosion on farms far away from markets was a greater national economic loss than erosion on close-in farms. Capital costs were also excluded because they are an insignificant portion of the total cost.

As for application costs, it takes a worker about four days to apply one ton of fertilizer

Table B-7. Value of Fertilizer and Agricultural Labor Used to Determine Cost of Soil Erosion in Costa Rica (1984 prices)

Year	Urea (price/mt)		Triple Super-phosphate (price/mt)		Potassium Muriate (price/mt)		Agricultural labor (cost/day)	
	Colones	US$	Colones	US$	Colones	US$	Colones	US$
1970	11,940	268.1	12,350	277.3	9,126	204.9	428	9.6
1971	11,032	247.7	11,411	256.2	8,432	189.4	437	9.8
1972	11,420	256.4	11,812	265.2	8,729	196.0	427	9.6
1973	11,758	264.0	12,161	273.1	8,987	201.8	401	9.0
1974	18,203	408.8	18,828	422.8	13,913	312.4	360	8.1
1975	16,369	367.6	16,931	380.2	12,512	281.0	352	7.9
1976	13,069	293.5	13,517	303.5	9,989	224.3	370	8.3
1977	12,648	284.0	13,082	293.8	9,667	217.1	384	8.6
1978	10,911	245.0	12,801	287.5	9,460	212.4	410	9.2
1979	13,682	307.2	13,433	301.6	9,927	222.9	392	8.8
1980	14,064	315.8	14,943	335.6	11,043	248.0	375	8.4
1981	12,645	283.9	14,985	336.5	11,073	248.7	278	6.3
1982	13,881	311.7	14,619	328.3	10,803	242.6	237	5.3
1983	12,272	275.6	11,916	267.6	8,805	197.7	279	6.3
1984	12,407	278.6	12,833	288.2	9,483	212.9	304	6.8
1985	13,351	299.8	13,950	313.2	10,308	231.5	332	7.5
1986	9,671	217.2	12,798	287.4	9,457	212.4	352	7.9
1987	8,743	196.3	11,570	259.8	8,549	192.0	360	8.1
1988	10,324	231.8	12,444	279.4	8,827	198.2	345	7.7
1989	10,715	240.6	12,610	283.2	8,945	200.9	371	8.3

Sources: Prices of potassium muriate and triple super-phosphate for 1985–88 and urea for 1978–88, were based on statistics from Jorge Campos, FERTICA, pers. com. (1990). The remaining years were estimated using the wholesale price index for fertilizers, Central Bank of Costa Rica, unpublished data.

(A. Vásquez, pers. com., 1990). The unit cost of labor was extrapolated from the 1989 value of ¢371/day, using the minimum wage index for agricultural labor.

For fertilizers, the resale price of FERTICA S.A. was used. Actual prices were obtained for 1978–89 (Jorge Orózco, pers. com., 1990). For years when the price varied, a weighted average was taken based on the number of months a price was in use.[29]

Results: Physical Accounts

Figure B-1 shows the total non-sustainable soil loss over the two decades. A comparison of this figure with Table B-1 shows that agricultural expansion has been accompanied by ever-increasing soil erosion.

Pastures comprise the largest agricultural land use nationally, but they contribute less to total erosion than do annual crops. Pasture

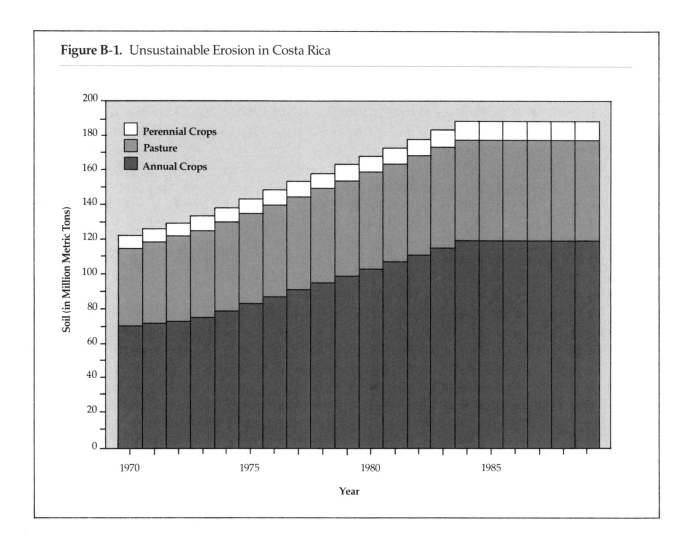

Figure B-1. Unsustainable Erosion in Costa Rica

Soil (in Million Metric Tons) (y-axis)

Perennial Crops
Pasture
Annual Crops

Year (x-axis)

areas have eroded at an estimated average rate of 33.8 mt/ha/yr, compared to the 289 mt/ha/yr for annual crops and 37.3 mt/ha/yr for perennial crops. Pasture lands, nonetheless, pose a significant land-use problem in Costa Rica.

First, the values used to estimate the total erosion are extremely conservative, and much more severe erosion in some areas is likely, particularly from deteriorated pastures where the surface cover has thinned out.[30]

Second, the methodology does not take into account other prevalent forms of soil deterioration, such as compaction and leaching.

Table B-8 gives an overview of erosion in Costa Rica. Table B-9 shows the total soil tonnage lost from 1970 to 1989, disaggregated for the three principal classes of land use.

Nationally, an estimated 2.2 billion mt of soil was eroded from 1970 to 1989—enough to cover the city of San José with 12 m of dirt. Most of this loss, 61.0 percent, occurred on land planted to annual crops. The remainder occurred on pasture (33.8 percent) and permanent crop lands (5.1 percent).

Table B-8. Overview of Erosion in Costa Rica (1984 values)

	Annual Crops	Perennial Crops	Pasture	Total or Average
Total tons lost (million mt)	125.5	14.2	84.4	224.1
Non-sustainable erosion (million mt)	119.3	9.4	59.9	188.6
Total area (thousand ha)	412.8	252.2	1,770.2	2,435.3
Total erosion/ha (mt)	304.0	56.3	47.6	92.0
Non-sustainable erosion/ha (mt)	289.0	37.3	33.8	77.4

Table B-9. Non-sustainable Erosion, by Land Use (million mt/yr)

Year	Annual Crops	Perennial Crops	Pasture	Total National Loss
1970	70.2	6.8	44.8	121.8
1971	72.0	6.9	46.6	125.5
1972	73.8	7.0	48.4	129.2
1973	75.6	7.2	50.1	132.9
1974	79.6	7.4	51.0	137.9
1975	83.5	7.6	51.9	143.0
1976	87.5	7.8	52.8	148.1
1977	91.5	8.0	53.7	153.1
1978	95.5	8.2	54.6	158.2
1979	99.4	8.4	55.4	163.3
1980	103.4	8.6	56.3	168.3
1981	107.4	8.8	57.2	173.4
1982	111.4	9.0	58.1	178.5
1983	115.3	9.2	59.0	183.5
1984	119.3	9.4	59.9	188.6
1985	119.3	9.4	59.9	188.6
1986	119.3	9.4	59.9	188.6
1987	119.3	9.4	59.9	188.6
1988	119.3	9.4	59.9	188.6
1989	119.3	9.4	59.9	188.6

Results: Economic Accounts

The economic depreciation per hectare for each of the three uses is presented in Table B-10. The decline in cost per hectare (in con-stant colones) reflects the overall reduction in resale fertilizer prices and the fall in real wages. *(See Table B-7.)*

The greatest loss per hectare is in soils planted to annual crops where nutrient concentrations are also highest. However, due to its vast area, pasture is also a major source of erosion. Perennial crops, mainly coffee and sugar cane, do not appear to have led to serious economic losses. *(See Table B-11.)*

During the period studied, the value of nutrients lost through erosion was significant—between 6.5 percent and 13.3 percent of the annual value added in agriculture.

Comparing erosion loss to the value of production, perennial crops bring the best return with the least erosion, only 0.3 tons of soil for each thousand colones of product. *(See Table B-12.)* For each thousand colones of product generated from pastures, the nation loses an average of 8.1 tons of soil worth 136.5 colones, over 13 percent of the value of the final product. For annual crops, erosion losses average 17 percent of the output value.

Table B-10. Average Depreciation of Soil Resource in Costa Rica by Land Use (1984 colones/ha)

Year	Annual Crops	Perennial Crops	Pasture	National Average
1970	4,008.5	502.3	527.9	1,022.4
1971	3,798.0	473.0	499.1	962.4
1972	3,947.1	488.7	517.5	993.8
1973	3,195.0	443.1	592.9	1,046.2
1974	4,888.2	664.5	866.7	1,566.0
1975	4,591.5	613.0	779.9	1,441.3
1976	3,891.6	511.1	634.9	1,198.5
1977	3,921.4	507.3	615.8	1,186.3
1978	3,603.9	460.2	545.7	1,072.0
1979	4,468.4	562.8	654.1	1,308.4
1980	4,708.2	586.5	667.0	1,358.1
1981	4,301.5	530.6	590.7	1,223.3
1982	4,722.8	576.4	629.9	1,325.3
1983	4,348.8	525.6	564.0	1,204.9
1984	4,542.9	544.7	573.4	1,243.4
1985	4,898.2	587.4	618.3	1,340.6
1986	3,746.9	450.1	472.7	1,025.4
1987	3,443.4	413.6	434.4	942.3
1988	3,935.0	472.3	496.5	1,076.9
1989	3,862.4	460.0	488.7	1,057.6

The real sustainable level of agricultural production, therefore, is the gross agricultural value added *less* the depreciation of the soil resource. Table B-13 shows the resulting net agricultural product.

During the period studied, the value of nutrients lost through erosion was significant—between 6.5 percent and 13.3 percent of the annual value added in agriculture. Continued erosion at this rate will keep national soil productivity from growing as fast as it should because soils left behind are poorer at deeper depths. Not even technological improvements and ready supplies of fertilizers will offset this constant decline in soil quality.

Economic Depreciation from Off-Site Erosion

Erosion has on-site and off-site effects. The off-site effects cited by Gregersen and associates (1988, p. 16) include:

- increases in sedimentation. This leads to productivity increases on alluvial plains from new deposits and soil banks; navigation restrictions; loss of reservoir capacity and increases in flooding frequency

Table B-11. Depreciation of Soil Resource in Costa Rica by Land Use (million 1984 colones)

Year	Annual Crops	Perennial Crops	Pasture	Total	Year	Annual Crops	Perennial Crops	Pasture	Total
1970	1,086.5	100.1	753.3	1,939.9	1980	1,853.5	143.9	1,090.2	3,087.7
1971	1,045.0	95.5	734.1	1,874.5	1981	1,714.0	131.1	985.4	2,830.6
1972	1,102.1	99.9	783.8	1,985.8	1982	1,904.5	143.4	1,072.2	3,120.1
1973	1,150.7	103.5	827.9	2,082.2	1983	1,774.5	131.7	979.2	2,885.4
1974	1,784.0	156.4	239.7	3,180.1	1984	1,875.4	137.4	1,015.1	3,027.9
1975	1,697.7	145.3	1,142.1	2,985.1	1985	2,022.1	148.1	1,094.5	3,264.7
1976	1,457.5	122.0	951.3	2,530.8	1986	1,546.8	113.5	836.7	2,497.0
1977	1,487.4	121.9	943.6	2,553.0	1987	1,421.6	104.3	769.0	2,294.8
1978	1,384.3	111.4	854.8	2,350.5	1988	1,624.5	119.1	879.0	2,622.5
1979	1,737.7	137.2	1,046.8	2,921.7	1989	1,594.5	116.0	865.1	2,575.6

Table B-12. Soil Resource Depreciation in Costa Rica—Economic Productivity Measure (1984 values)

	Annual Crops	Perennial Crops	Pasture	All Land Uses
Non-sustainable erosion/ha (tons)	289.0	37.3	33.8	77.4
Value of soil loss/ha (1984 colones)	4,542.9	544.7	573.4	1,243.4
Economic production/ha (thousand 1984 colones)	26.3	123.6	4.2	15.8
Tons of erosion per thousand colones of economic product	11.0	0.3	8.1	4.9
Depreciation per thousand colones of economic product (1984 colones)	172.7	4.4	136.5	78.7

Note: Economic productivity per ha was calculated by dividing the total value of production by the area under each crop.

Sources: Economic productivity: Banco Central de Costa Rica, *Cifras sobre producción agropecuaria 1978–1987,* Departamento de Contabilidad Social, San José, Costa Rica, 1989. Crop area: Dirección General de Estadística y Censos, *Censo Agropecuario—1984,* San José, Costa Rica, 1987.

• modifications in the water regime. Water availability diminishes in critical periods. Irrigation, transport capability, and hydroelectric generation capacity are curtailed, and fresh water fisheries are endangered

• changes in water quality.

The productivity of hydroelectric plants and irrigation systems are not adequately considered in the current system of national accounts.

Water. Erosion takes a toll on a nation's hydroelectric generation capacity in at least two ways. First, it reduces the useful life of existing generating systems. In this case, sedimentation cost *equals* the *difference* between the real value of the system's useful life (taking real sedimentation into account) and the value of the designed useful life.

Second, erosion reduces untapped electricity generation potential. Watersheds lose energy potential with erosion, changes in the water regime, shifts in plant cover, and the build-up of sediment in the river bed. Although the available potential is unutilized, it can be assigned a value:

$$(4) \quad DPPE_u = \frac{DE_u \cdot VRE_u}{i(1+i)^m},$$

where:

$DPPE_u$ = depreciation due to the loss in potential energy generation in year u,

DE_u = loss of energy generation potential through erosion in year u,

VRE_u = rent value per unit of energy in year u,

i = interest rate, and

m = year energy use would begin.

Irrigation Systems. Through its immediate impact on the water regime, erosion limits a region's irrigation potential. By projecting

Table B-13. Value Added to Agriculture, Gross and Net of Soil Depreciation
(million 1984 colones)

Year	Value Added in Agriculture[a]	Soil Depreciation	Adjusted Net Value of Agriculture	Depreciation as Percent of Agricultural Value Added
1970	21,044	1,940	19,104.	9.2%
1971	19,277	1,875	17,403	9.7%
1972	20,278	1,986	18,292	9.8%
1973	23,570	2,082	21,488	8.8%
1974	23,835	3,180	20,655	13.3%
1975	25,503	2,985	22,518	11.7%
1976	26,960	2,531	24,429	9.4%
1977	31,513	2,553	28,960	8.1%
1978	31,258	2,350	28,908	7.5%
1979	29,713	2,922	26,792	9.8%
1980	28,668	3,088	25,580	10.8%
1981	36,804	2,831	33,973	7.7%
1982	35,220	3,120	32,100	8.9%
1983	33,679	2,885	30,794	8.6%
1984	34,540	3,028	31,512	8.8%
1985	31,879	3,265	28,614	10.2%
1986	37,057	2,497	34,560	6.7%
1987	33,615	2,295	31,320	6.8%
1988	37,309	2,623	34,687	7.0%
1989	39,459	2,576	36,883	6.5%

a. BCCR Banco Central de Costa Rica, *Cifras sobre producción agropecuaria 1978–87*, San José, 1989, and *Estadísticas 1950–1985*, 1986; and unpublished BCCR data.

annual rates of potential production loss, the loss of future rents due to erosion can be estimated.

Depreciation through loss of irrigation capacity equals the actualized value of the difference in rents from land with and without irrigation. When this potential is not for immediate but future use, depreciation can be calculated as:

$$(5) \quad DIC_u = \frac{IC_u \cdot DRT_u \cdot PIC_u}{i(1+i)^m},$$

where:

DIC_u = depreciation due to loss of irrigation capacity in year u,

IC_u = original irrigation capacity of watershed, in hectares, in year u,

PIC_u = percentage decline in irrigation capacity due to erosion in year u,

DRT = difference in land rents with and without irrigation,

m = year surface area would have been irrigated, and

i = interest rate.

Irrigable area lost to erosion is hard to estimate and evaluate for depreciation. Its value could turn out to be large because agricultural potential in many zones depends on access to water.

Off-site Effects of Soil Erosion: An Example

Costa Rica depends on hydroelectric energy for 99 percent of its electricity needs. Even though deforestation and erosion take an obvious economic toll on national electricity generating systems (Leonard, 1986), rarely do designs for hydroelectric projects incorporate adequate natural resource management provisions (Rodríguez, 1989). Data are badly needed to evaluate and compare the cost of integrated loss-prevention management with the cost of erosion losses in electricity generating systems.

As an example, Rodríguez (1989) analyzed how deforestation and erosion affected the capacity of the Cachí dam in the upper Reventazón watershed. This hydroelectric project has a 323.6 ha reservoir and a storage capacity of 54 million m³. The reservoir is managed so that it is full at the end of the rainy season, and the plant can generate energy at full capacity during the dry season.

This project depends on water from the upper Reventazón River. The watershed has a total surface area of 795.6 km², 78 percent of it on slopes steeper than 30 percent. The generating plant, which began operating in 1966, today has an installed capacity of 100,800 kw and produces an average of 587,000 mwh/yr (Rodríguez, 1989 p. 96). This is 15 percent of Costa Rica's annual electricity production, and, based on national hydroelectric energy costs, has a value of ¢110.7 million (US$2.2 million).[31]

Rodríguez (1989) showed that sedimentation has considerably altered the river basin. Previous observation had indicated that the project was at risk (Leonard, 1986). For example, between 1956 and 1984, an estimated 166 km² of the watershed was deforested, reducing forest cover from 60.2 percent to 43.1 percent of the total area. At the same time, conversions to cattle pasture increased from 20 percent to 34 percent of the surface area. Rodríguez also found 25 percent of the basin in varying states of degradation.

Methodology. Rodríguez's methodology compared the upper basin of the Reventazón River during a period of low overuse and substantial land-use changes in 1953–69, with a period of more intense overuse but fewer modifications in plant coverage in 1970–86. The second period coincided with the creation of the Rio Macho Forestry Reserve, which afforded the area better protection. The effects of land use on river regimes and reservoir sedimentation were determined for both periods, and their economic value was estimated.

The effects of the land use changes upon the minimum, maximum, and average river flow rates were first determined. The quantity of the sediments carried by the river were then calculated, using measurements of sediment rates and the estimated flow rates. The total sediment deposits in the reservoir could then be established, taking into account the characteristics of the reservoir and river currents.

Having determined the accumulation of sediment within the reservoir, it was possible to calculate the reduction in available energy. The costs of replacing this lost energy with thermal and imported sources were then calculated to yield the cost borne by the project, due to the changes in land use.

Results. The effects of the land use changes on the Reventazón basin and the Cachí Dam can be summarized as follows:

- Maximum water volumes grew from 1953 to 1966, but have declined every year since then.

- The mean volumes grew until 1968 and then began to decline—a trend typical of areas where vegetative cover is changing. (Hamilton and King, 1983).

- The average minimum volumes do not show any significant variation over time between the two periods. Nevertheless, the variability of the minimum volumes increased from the first to the second period.

- The average annual rate of sedimentation in the reservoir increased 73 percent between the first and the second periods (Rodríguez, 1989, p. 100).

Comparing the two periods, during and after alterations in ground cover, the following costs were defined:

- The loss due to the reduction of energy attributable to diminished flow at the dam was estimated at ¢1.91 million/yr, the value of the alternative costs of thermal production and electricity importation.

- Work stoppages at the plant for dredging, an average of 15 days/yr, were valued at ¢3.77 million/yr.

- Increased maintenance costs caused due to sedimentation were estimated at ¢8.48 million/yr.

Thus, the annual losses attributable to sedimentation amounted to ¢14.5 million/yr (US$287,000) 13 percent of the annual production value. The expansion of cattle ranching and agriculture in the Reventazón River basin has caused a significant depreciation in the productive value of the Cachí hydroelectric plant. This depreciation was not reflected in the national accounts when deforestation occurred, but shows up today as lower revenue from the plant and higher charges for Costa Rican consumers.

C. Fishery Accounts

Overview: Costa Rican Fisheries

Costa Rican fisheries are characterized by species diversity and a heterogeneous fleet. Most fishing is done for relatively small local markets. Although of limited importance to the national economy, in some regions fishing and canning are the main sources of employment. Overfishing thus jeopardizes the local fishing industry's stability.

Fish products have traditionally provided protein for the subsistence communities on Costa Rica's shores, especially on the Pacific Coast where marine resources are more abundant. Fishing remained a subsistence activity until the second half of the 19th century, when commercial fishing began in the Gulf of Nicoya. The industrialization of Costa Rica's fishing began when Spanish immigrants arrived with new fishing technology. The canning of tuna caught by foreign boats began in the 1940s. By the late 1970s, three sardine canneries, supplied primarily by the domestic fleet, were operating on the Pacific coast.

Costa Rica's fishing fleet operates at three levels of technology: artisanal, semi-industrial, and industrial. The artisanal fleet has many types of vessels, from simple rowboats to ships that can stay at sea for a week or two. In 1987, some 6,600 fishermen operated roughly 2,200 artisanal boats in Costa Rica (NORAD/FAO/OLDEPESCA, 1990, p. 75). The semi-industrial fleet consists mainly of 90 shrimp boats, employing 800 fishermen. The industrial fleet supplies the national canneries with fish and exports fresh and frozen fish. Today, all industrial boats under the Costa Rican flag are foreign owned. The 1987 harvests by each technology are presented in Figure C-1.

In 1987, fishing contributed less than 1 percent of the gross domestic product and only 3.8 percent of the agricultural product *(See Table C-1.)* These values were, respectively, five and six times larger than in 1970. Policies

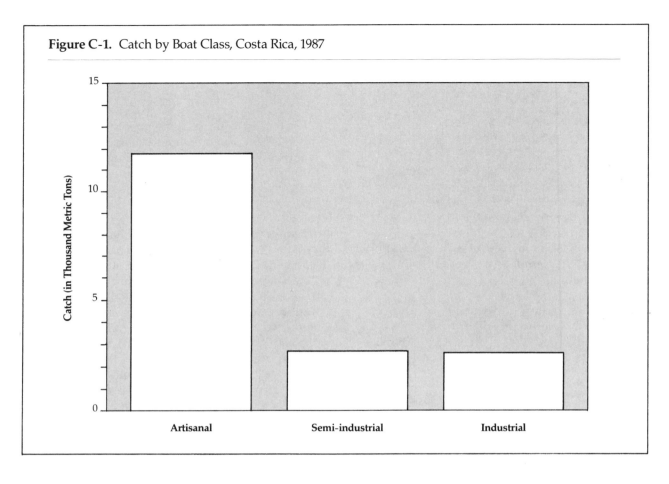

Figure C-1. Catch by Boat Class, Costa Rica, 1987

Catch (in Thousand Metric Tons)

15

10

5

0

Artisanal   Semi-industrial   Industrial

designed to transform fishing into a major economic activity (such as tax forgiveness on inputs in 1970 and preferential fuel prices and tax certificates in 1984) have increased revenue, but at the expense of the underlying fishery resource.

During the 1950s and 1960s, the fish harvest grew slowly in Costa Rica, averaging only 3,466 metric tons annually.[32] *(See Figure C-2.)* However, the 1970s witnessed an abrupt increase in fishery production, from 7,000 mt in 1970 to 21,000 in 1978. Total production dropped off sharply around 1980, to less than half the 1978 level by 1983. After 1983, fish yields recovered, reaching 16,000 mt by 1986.

Looking at individual species, problems in the fishing sector are easier to see. Catches of

highly valued white and fidel shrimp, for example, declined by 70 percent and 90 percent, respectively, between 1985 and 1988. Sardine production peaked in 1975 at 7,500 mt before dropping to 507 mt in 1987. Large, first-grade fish production declined from an average of 360,000 mt from 1982 to 1984 to 236,000 mt from 1985 to 1987.

Yields have varied dramatically over the past 20 years, although the fishing fleet has grown larger and its technology more sophisticated.[33] This combination of shrinking catches and increasing numbers of fishing vessels is symptomatic of overfishing.

Two species-specific studies have confirmed overfishing in the Gulf of Nicoya. Madrigal (1985) used electronic length-frequency analysis

Table C-1. Value Added by Fishery Sector to GDP and to Agricultural Product

Year	Million 1984 Colones	Million 1984 US$	Fish as % of GDP	Fish as % of Ag. GDP
1970	117.5	2.6	0.13%	0.56%
1971	138.5	3.1	0.15%	0.72%
1972	138.2	3.1	0.14%	0.68%
1973	162.6	3.7	0.14%	0.69%
1974	196.7	4.4	0.16%	0.83%
1975	196.2	4.4	0.16%	0.77%
1976	243.6	5.5	0.18%	0.90%
1977	218.6	4.9	0.15%	0.69%
1978	567.0	12.7	0.37%	1.94%
1979	763.0	17.1	0.48%	1.34%
1980	640.8	14.4	0.40%	1.16%
1981	652.3	14.6	0.41%	1.01%
1982	751.3	16.9	0.51%	1.37%
1983	585.7	13.2	0.38%	1.15%
1984	865.3	19.4	0.53%	1.88%
1985	1,268.2	28.5	0.75%	1.28%
1986	1,225.4	27.5	0.69%	2.74%
1987	1,465.9	32.9	0.79%	3.79%

Source: Banco Central de Costa Rica, *Cifras sobre producción agropecuaria 1978–1987*, Departamento de Contabilidad Social, San José, 1989; *Estadísticas 1950–1985*, Division Económica, San José, 1986; and unpublished data.

(ELEFAN) to analyze three species of *Corvina* in 1979 and 1982. ELEFAN does not reveal stock levels or maximum sustainable catch size, but it does provide important management indicators. The exploitation ratio—fishing mortality (catches), *divided* by total mortality (harvests plus natural deaths)—can be used as an indicator of harvesting beyond replacement level. For two of the three *Corvina* species studied (*C. aguada* and *C. agria*), the exploitation ratio increased from 0.48 and 0.41 in 1979 to 0.55 and 0.51 in 1982. According to Pauly (1980, p. 30), an exploitation ratio of 0.5 is optimal. When fishing mortality exceeds natural mortalities, forcing the ratio above 0.5, the stock is probably being overexploited.

Stevenson and Carranza (1981) analyzed sardine yields *(Opisthonema spp.)* per unit of effort in the Gulf of Nicoya. Using a logarithmic surplus production model, the authors demonstrated that the maximum sustainable level of effort was exceeded three years during the sardine industry boom in the late 1970s. As yield dropped off, so did the profitability of the fleet. Both effort and production declined dramatically as a result.

Three indicators of fishery resource depletion are evident: a decline in total fishery productivity, a reduced proportion of high-valued species in the total catch, and an increase in the number of boats fishing the area. Contaminants in the coastal waters, particularly in the Gulf of Nicoya, are also believed to have harmed the fishing industry and have been linked to the decline in the local shrimp harvests.[34] This effect cannot yet be quantified,

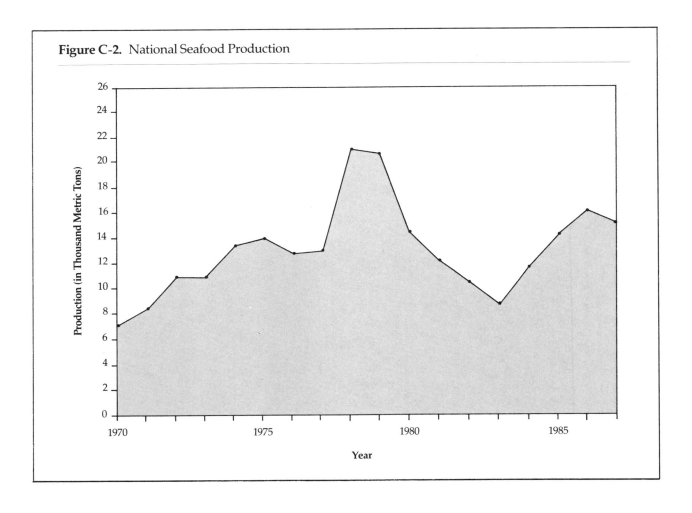

Figure C-2. National Seafood Production

(y-axis: Production (in Thousand Metric Tons); x-axis: Year)

however, because neither contaminant volume nor their link to the biological cycle have yet been ascertained precisely.

Depreciation of Fishery Resources

Any fishery is prey to diverse natural pressures. Climate determines not only species mix but also growth and reproduction rates. Currents, changes in surrounding ecosystems, and a multitude of other naturally occurring phenomena can cause dramatic fluctuations in yields. Fishery dynamics become much more complicated when fishing begins. With limited fishing, reproduction rates increase, but at high harvest rates, the stock can be virtually fished out of existence. The human presence also

affects the productivity of the fish stock by altering water quality, destroying coastal ecosystems, or disrupting the food chain.[35]

Fish cannot be counted directly, so stocks are usually assessed indirectly through quantitative modeling. If all other factors remain constant, the fishery biomass will decline as fishing efforts increase.

The correlation between fishing effort, f, and sustainable yields in tropical fisheries normally takes the curve shown in Figure C-3.[36] At low levels of fishing effort, increases in fishing decrease the total fish stock, allowing faster growth. As a result, sustainable yields increase. The maximum sustainable yield *(MSY)* occurs

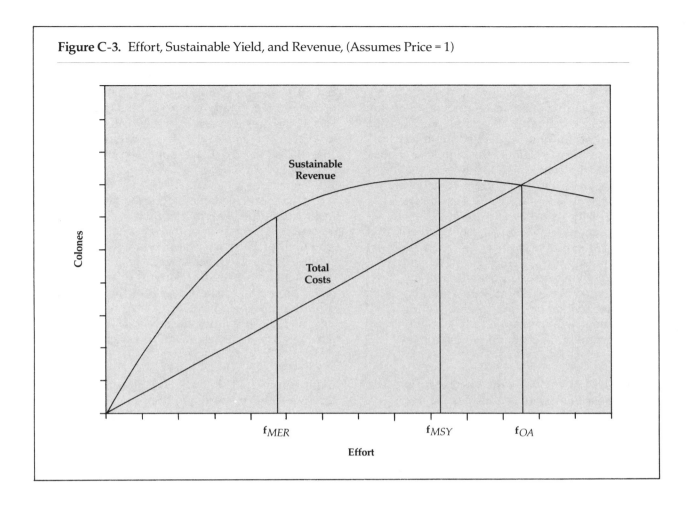

Figure C-3. Effort, Sustainable Yield, and Revenue, (Assumes Price = 1)

Colones

Sustainable
Revenue

Total
Costs

f_{MER} f_{MSY} f_{OA}

Effort

at the point denominated by f_{MSY}. Once f_{MSY} is reached, however, further increases in fishing effort will reduce yields because increased exploitation leads to the capture of fish before they reach their optimal harvest size. If overfishing is severe, harvesting fish before they reach reproductive age can cause the fishery to collapse.

The economic optimum occurs at that point where the rents generated by the harvest are maximized.[37] Assuming that costs are linearly variable with effort and that prices are constant, the yield curve *(Figure C-3)* becomes a revenue curve, and total costs can be represented as a straight line from the origin. The sustainable economic rent from each level of effort *equals* the vertical distance between the

curves at that level of effort. At the point labeled f_{MER}, maximum sustainable economic rents *(MER)* are reached.

A fishery, like any other asset, can be valued as the present value of potential future rents—that is, the discounted value of the stream of future incomes *less* all costs. The model described above shows the correlation between effort and sustainable harvests. In a static model, where effort is assumed to remain constant at level t, the asset value of the fishery, V_{fr}, would be the capitalized value of the sustainable rents generated by that effort. This can be expressed as:

$$V_{fr} = (I_t - C_t)/i,$$

where I_t and C_t are the incomes and costs (including the cost of capital) attributable to a given level of effort, t, and i is the prevailing discount rate.

In a simple dynamic model, the value of the asset would be equal to the rents that could be generated ad infinitum by adjusting effort to maximize returns. Neither the simple dynamic model nor the static model, however, accurately describes the normal behavior of effort levels in open-access (OA) fisheries. Effort actually rises beyond the MER level because rents for individual fishermen still exist until f_{OA}, even though fisheries' economic rents are maximized at f_{MER}. In Figure C-3, individual rents will always be positive until average returns equal average cost at f_{OA}. As long as alternative livelihoods are limited, fishing employment will increase, leading to the effort level f_{OA} where all economic rents are dissipated.[38]

The Gulf of Nicoya in the northwest is Costa Rica's most heavily fished locality. It has 64 percent of the fleet[39] and produces 32 percent of the yields.[40] Because most vessels fishing the Gulf are small, fishing there is done mainly in one-day trips. Vessels more than 10-m long are not allowed to operate inside the Gulf.

Shrimp, sardines, and a wide variety of demersal species are caught in and around the Gulf of Nicoya. As shown in Table C-2, the artisanal fleet is the main source of pressure upon the shark and fish species.

Data Sources and Estimates

The first step in fishery resource valuation is estimating the sustainable yield curve of the resource. Building on Fox (1970) and Silvestre and Pauly (1986), the yield curve for the Gulf of Nicoya stocks is estimated:

$$(1) \quad Y/f \;=\; e^{(a+bf)}$$

where Y is the annual yield and f is an estimate of fishing effort.

Yield data have been collected, with varying degrees of accuracy, since the early 1950s by the Fishery and Aquaculture Service (Dirección General de Recursos Pesqueros y Acuacultura, DGRP). As shown in Figure C-4, while total yields varied greatly due to booms and busts in particular species, demersal fish catches (*pescado* and shark) rose more or less constantly during the 1970s. The 1980s were marked by greater variability.

No data are available before the late 1980s for estimating directly fishing effort in Costa Rica except a 1989 census of the artisanal fleet in the Gulf of Nicoya. Information about the physical characteristics of each boat in the fleet was obtained, including length, type of gear used, and construction date. On the assumption that any boat built since 1970 was still in use in 1989, the number of vessels and their characteristics was estimated for each year.

Only 28 boats in the 1989 census had been built before 1971, but about 275 boats are known to have been operating in 1970 (Fernando Viquez, DGRP, pers. com., 1990). To account for this discrepancy, 247 vessels were added to the 1970 fleet, for a total of 275. The characteristics of the total fleet in 1970 were assumed to be the same as those for the pre-1971 boats still in operation in 1989. The 247 boats added to the 1970 fleet were assumed to have been retired from service at a constant rate of 13 a year from 1971 to 1988. Both the unadjusted and adjusted total fleet values are presented in Table C-3.[41]

The census of artisanal fishermen counted three main types of boats; *botes, pangas,* and *lanchas.* Botes and pangas are both simple craft. (More than half of the botes in the census were oar powered; pangas are larger and almost always powered by an outboard motor.) Based on a sample of DGRP daily catch records from 1990, the fishing efficiency of an oar-powered bote was 75 percent that of a 1-kw bote.[42] Accordingly, botes without motors were assigned a power equivalent of 0.75 kw. Lanchas are larger, more powerful, and able to fish

Table C-2. Seafood Catch by Artisanal Fleet, Gulf of Nicoya (metric tons)

Year	Fish Total Gulf Catch	Fish Artisanal Catch (percent)	Sharks Total Gulf Catch	Sharks Artisanal Catch (percent)	Shrimp[a] Total Gulf Catch	Shrimp[a] Artisanal Catch (percent)	Sardines[a] Total Gulf Catch	Sardines[a] Artisanal Catch (percent)
1970	732	89.0%	102	47.5%	795	—	1,883	—
1971	971	61.3%	100	80.8%	1,007	—	1,662	—
1972	1,074	52.6%	89	71.7%	790	—	2,912	—
1973	1,362	78.4%	152	95.0%	838	—	2,926	—
1974	1,775	83.4%	209	100.2%[b]	841	—	4,313	—
1975	1,736	88.8%	247	108.1%[b]	808	—	4,492	—
1976	1,872	87.9%	192	79.1%	784	—	3,798	—
1977	2,019	81.9%	211	75.8%	376	—	3,212	—
1978	2,387	67.0%	238	79.4%	371	—	2,876	—
1979	2,170	75.6%	256	86.1%	626	—	2,190	—
1980	2,422	81.6%	187	76.3%	595	—	2,183	—
1981	1,863	76.5%	203	99.8%	660	—	734	—
1982	2,439	71.4%	162	84.4%	818	—	627	—
1983	2,821	70.6%	206	89.0%	442	—	729	—
1984	2,490	92.0%	156	71.1%	913	—	1,569	—
1985	2,671	88.0%	179	88.3%	2,051	—	815	—
1986	2,904	93.7%	128	81.4%	1,309	—	1,307	—
1987	2,444	122.1%[b]	179	99.0%	1,230	—	425	—
1988	1,899	68.3%	125	91.1%	786	7.3%	553	4.5%

— Not available.

Source: Dirección General de Recursos Pesqueros y Acuacultura, San José, Costa Rica, unpublished data.

a. Data on artisanal catches are available only for 1988.
b. Due to the presence of values over 100 percent, the artisanal production data were deemed unreliable and are excluded from the statistical analysis.

for a number of days at a time. All three boat types are used commercially because distances within the Gulf are not great. Pangas, which are well suited for Gulf shrimp fishing, have become increasingly popular since shrimp fishing was legalized in the mid-1980s.

From the census data, yearly fleet power could be calculated. Each type of vessel, however, has a different fishing efficiency, and hence puts a different degree of pressure on the resource. To obtain a standard unit of fish-

ing effort, all power estimates had to be converted to a standard unit: *lancha-kw.*

Table C-4 presents the formulas used to convert kilowatts of power into the lancha equivalents. In 1988, the DGRP recorded a large sample of daily boat catches by type of artisanal boat. By dividing the sampled harvest of each boat type, in line (B), by the total unadjusted kilowatts in the 1988 fleet, in line (A), an index of the relative efficiency per unit of power of both classes of boat was obtained. The fishing

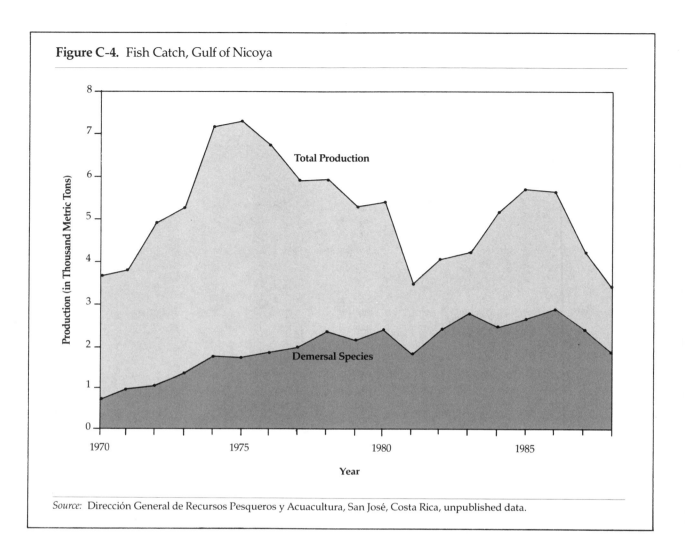

Figure C-4. Fish Catch, Gulf of Nicoya

Source: Dirección General de Recursos Pesqueros y Acuacultura, San José, Costa Rica, unpublished data.

efficiency per unit of small boat power relative to that of large boat power was 1.27. To estimate the portion of total effort used by each boat class for fishing pescado and shark (as opposed to shrimp or sardines), the ratio of total effort devoted to catching a particular type of fish was assumed to be the same as that type's contribution to total revenue. Again, using the 1988 data, the total revenue from fishing were obtained for the sample, and the percentage of total revenue provided by fishing was found to be 55.5 percent for small boats and 77.4 percent for large boats. Multiplying fishing efficiency relative to *lancha* effi-

ciency [line (C) divided by 63.77 or line (C) for lanchas] by the proportion of total effort put into fishing (D), the factor used to convert standard kilowatts to lancha-kw of fishing power was obtained, line (E). The overall pressure upon the resource per unit of power was assumed to remain constant during the entire period.

Based on this adjustment factor, total lancha-kw were calculated for the fleet for each year from 1970 to 1989. *(See Table C-5.)* To smooth out the series, three-year averages of the fishing effort were used.

Table C-3. Number of Estimated Artisanal Fishing Vessels Operating in the Gulf of Nicoya

| | Direct Interpretation of Census | | | | Census, *plus* 247-boat adjustment for 1970 | | | |
Year	Botes	Pangas	Lanchas	Total	Botes	Pangas	Lanchas	Total
1970	13	6	9	28	128	59	88	275
1971	15	6	11	32	124	56	86	266
1972	25	6	12	43	128	53	83	264
1973	39	6	16	61	136	51	83	270
1974	48	7	21	76	139	49	83	271
1975	67	11	27	105	152	50	85	287
1976	97	12	36	145	176	48	90	314
1977	117	14	47	178	190	47	97	334
1978	197	17	76	290	264	48	122	434
1979	254	18	88	360	315	46	130	491
1980	319	24	130	473	373	49	167	589
1981	353	30	141	524	401	52	174	627
1982	400	38	166	604	442	58	195	695
1983	457	51	194	702	493	68	219	780
1984	518	70	226	814	548	84	247	879
1985	582	117	253	952	606	128	270	1,004
1986	628	198	282	1,108	646	206	294	1,146
1987	661	339	299	1,299	673	345	307	1,325
1988	704	433	325	1,462	710	436	329	1,475
1989	706	456	330	1,492	706	456	330	1,492

Source: MAG, 1989 and Dirección General de Recursos Pesqueros y Acuacultura, San José, Costa Rica, Census of the Gulf of Nicoya, unpublished data (D-base) 1989.

Table C-4. Conversion Formulas, Small Vessels Power to Lancha-kw Units

	Botes and Pangas	Lanchas
(A) Total kw in 1988 fleet[a]	6,082.7	6,153.5
(B) Fish harvest in 1988 sample[b]	493,648	392,441
(C) Fish harvest per kw of fleet power	81.16	63.77
(D) Revenue obtained from fish (%)[b]	55.5%	77.4%
(E) Lancha-kw of fishing power per standard kw $[(C)/(C_L))^2 \, (D)]$	0.71	0.77

a. Based on calculations using unpublished data from the Dirección General de Recursos Pesqueros y Acuacultura, San José and MAG, Ministerio de Agricultura y Ganadería (1989).
b. Based on 1988 production data, by type of vessel.

Table C-5. Artisanal Fishing Effort, Gulf of Nicoya

	Power of Adjusted Fleet (kw)				Fishing Power (lancha-kw)			
Year	Botes	Pangas	Lanchas	Total	Small	Medium	Total	Three year Average
1970	180	315	852	1,347	350	659	1,009	1,009
1971	176	300	848	1,324	336	657	993	1,001
1972	199	285	813	1,297	342	629	971	991
1973	225	270	828	1,323	350	641	991	985
1974	237	256	866	1,359	349	670	1,018	993
1975	254	261	869	1,385	364	673	1,037	1,015
1976	311	265	930	1,506	407	720	1,126	1,060
1977	347	261	1,136	1,744	429	879	1,309	1,157
1978	507	260	1,395	2,162	542	1,080	1,622	1,352
1979	595	251	1,474	2,319	597	1,140	1,738	1,556
1980	741	311	3,258	4,311	743	2,521	3,265	2,208
1981	793	334	3,321	4,449	796	2,570	3,367	2,790
1982	908	372	3,562	4,842	904	2,757	3,661	3,431
1983	1,013	493	4,061	5,567	1,064	3,142	4,206	3,744
1984	1,171	732	4,528	6,431	1,344	3,504	4,848	4,238
1985	1,437	1,158	4,910	7,506	1,833	3,800	5,633	4,896
1986	1,595	1,878	5,320	8,790	2,450	4,117	6,567	5,683
1987	1,675	3,225	5,695	10,596	3,461	4,400	7,868	6,689
1988	1,782	4,301	6,153	12,236	4,296	4,762	9,057	7,831
1989	1,786	4,524	6,201	12,511	4,456	4,798	9,254	8,726

Source: Calculations from Table C-4 and MAG, 1989.

Physical Accounts: Biomass and Maximum Sustainable Yield

Since only data on catch and effort are available over time, the conceptual relationship between fish biomass and catch per unit of effort was used to determine the trend in biomass decline during the period. With data from Madrigal (1985) on *corvina* biomass for 1979 and 1982, the likely range of biomass for the entire fish stock was projected for the 1970s and 1980s. *Corvina* comprise an estimated 35 percent to 55 percent of the total biomass (Madrigal, 1985), which is reflected in the range of possible biomass in Figure C-5.

These estimates were obtained in three steps. First, total biomass had to be estimated for at least one year. Madrigal (1985) estimated that the biomass of the three species of *Corvina* considered totaled 1,153.8 mt in 1979 and 983.5 mt in 1982. From 1977 to 1984, *corvina* represented between 43 percent and 55 percent of all harvests (Madrigal, pers. comm. 1990) These values were used to estimate a range of 2,098 mt to 3,297 mt for the total Gulf biomass in 1979.

Second, the correlation described by equation (1) can be rewritten in terms of F, fishing mortality and q, the catchability coefficient:

$$(2) \quad Y/(F/q) = e^{(a+bf)}.$$

Since fish biomass, $B = Y/F$, equation (2) can be expressed:

$$(3) \quad lnB = a + bf - lnq.[43]$$

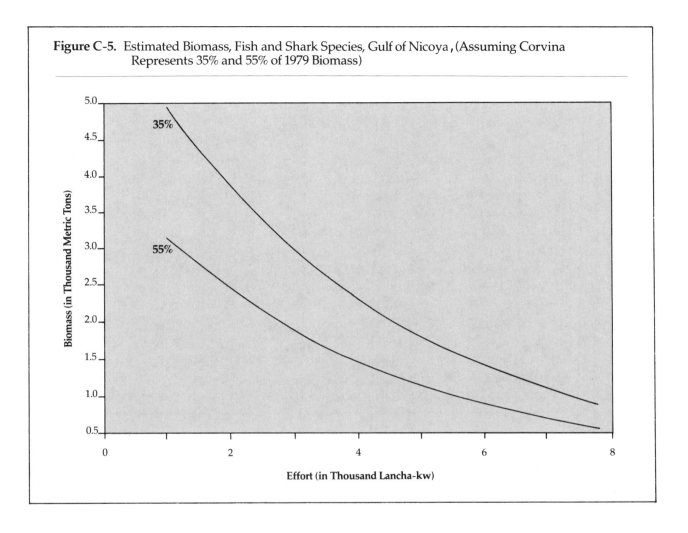

Figure C-5. Estimated Biomass, Fish and Shark Species, Gulf of Nicoya , (Assuming Corvina Represents 35% and 55% of 1979 Biomass)

Given the effort index developed in the previous section, the values for *a* and *b* derived in equation (4) and the range of biomass for 1979, equation (3) was solved for a range of *q* values. This was repeated for a range of biomass values for 1982, producing a second range of *q* values. The lower and upper limits of these two sets of *q* values were then averaged.

These averages for lower and upper limits of *q* were used in equation (3), together with estimates of *a* and *b* and annual data on *f*, to derive lower and upper limits for *B* for each year. The two downward sloping curves delimit the likely range for the Gulf's biomass. Figure C-5 shows that this declining biomass range has been associated with increasing fishing effort.

To estimate the fishery's sustainable yield, the index of fishing effort was regressed on the fish catch (DGRP classifications *pescado* and *tiburón*), using Fox's model,

(4) $\quad Y/f \;=\; e^{(7.80 \,-\, 0.000256 \cdot f)} .44$

Figure C-6 presents the estimated sustainable yield curve from the above equation. Yield levels include only the harvests of fish and sharks, specifically excluding shrimp and sardines (the other primary products in and around the Gulf), which are fished primarily by the semi-industrial fleet.

57

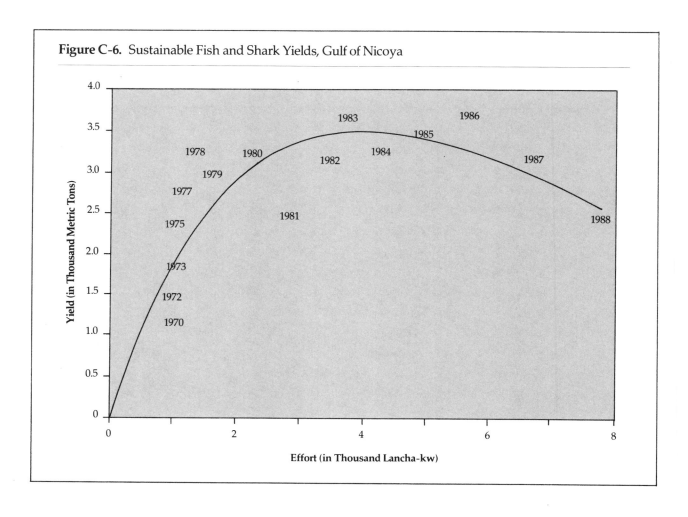

Figure C-6. Sustainable Fish and Shark Yields, Gulf of Nicoya

As the figure shows, the estimated maximum sustainable yield level for fishing in the Gulf of Nicoya was reached in 1983 at 3.51 thousand mt of fish from a fleet of 780 boats, equivalent to about 3.7 thousand lancha-kw. Only a few times have yields surpassed the estimated MSY level, and the sustainable harvest level has declined markedly since 1986. In a physical sense, therefore, Gulf fishing productivity will probably not reach its productive potential until total effort declines.

Economic Accounts: Depreciation

As demonstrated above, the value of a fishery *equals* the discounted present value of future sustainable rents for a particular level of effort. The annual return at any level of effort *equals* the sustainable yield *times* the average price, *less* total fishing costs.

The annual economic rent was determined by calculating price per unit of production and costs per unit of effort for each year in the period studied. *(See Table C-6.)* Prices were determined by taking a weighted average of the relevant fish-class prices from unpublished DGRP data.

Costs per unit of effort were estimated in three steps. Three individuals who worked closely with Gulf fishermen were interviewed

Table C-6. Cost and Price Data Used in Determining Annual Rents (current colones)

Year	Cost/ Lancha-kw	Average Price of Fish/kg[a]	Year	Cost/ Lancha-kw	Average Price of Fish/kg[a]
1970	1,177.8	2.2	1980	5,175.1	25.4
1971	1,258.2	2.4	1981	7,829.9	33.7
1972	1,309.2	2.9	1982	13,864.1	35.0
1973	1,463.4	3.6	1983	17,612.4	34.3
1974	1,975.7	3.8	1984	19,396.6	37.7
1975	2,328.0	4.7	1985	21,712.3	46.6
1976	2,591.1	5.5	1986	23,514.6	59.1
1977	2,831.1	6.9	1987	25,019.2	67.1
1978	3,181.9	8.7	1988	28,371.3	77.3
1979	3,720.1	11.3	1989	32,809.4	81.9

a. Price paid at port. *Source:* Dirección General de Recursos Pesqueros y Acuacultura, San José, Costa Rica, unpublished data.

to obtain estimates of the true operating costs of botes, pangas and lanchas.[45] Then daily and annual costs were estimated for 1990. Finally, capital assets were valued based on the annual interest on the original investment *plus* the cost of straight line depreciation of the asset.[46]

Total annual operating costs were calculated for the rest of the period, based on price indices. The results were converted into costs per lancha-kw of fishing effort by *dividing* by the average number of lancha-kw per boat type. Finally, a weighted average of the three boat types was taken, based upon the number of boats operating each year, to obtain the average annual unit cost per lancha-kw. *(See Table C-6.)*

Since gasoline and diesel fuel in the fishing sector are subsidized by government and available at below-market prices and since fishing supplies are exempt from Costa Rica's typically high import taxes, fishermen enjoy artificially low fishing costs—a stimulus to fleet expansion.

The economic returns to fishermen *equal* revenue *less* the opportunity cost of fishing. For a

number of reasons, this cost is difficult to estimate. The government-set minimum wage is a poor indicator in Costa Rica because unemployment and underemployment are higher in the Gulf than nationally. In 1989, national underemployment in agriculture, fishing, and forestry reached 18.7 percent (NORAD/FAO/OLDEPESCA, 1990), but, in 1984, unemployment rates were some 50 percent higher in the Gulf than the national average.[47] Employment as a farm laborer does not offer a fisherman a real alternative.

To reflect these conditions, the opportunity cost of labor was tied to the basic family support that government gives the unemployed. In 1990, this support program *(Bono Alimentario)* was equivalent to 7,500 colones a month, 71 percent of the minimum agricultural wage. This value was extrapolated to the rest of the period using the minimum wage index.

Fishermen's real input and operating outlays are often less than the total costs estimated above. Many (perhaps most) fishermen cannot keep up with their debts. Foreclosures on these loans are rare, however, because intermediaries often lend fishermen money, with no expectation of repayment, in exchange for their loyalty. Thus assured of a cheap and steady supply, these entrepreneurs can make large profits transporting fish to market. Furthermore, because fishermen often neglect maintenance, not all of their operating costs are on the books (Carlos Villalobos, pers. com., 1991). Consequently, fishermen do not take into account the full cost of capital.

Gulf of Nicoya

To calculate the total revenue and cost curves, annual cost and price values were applied to the entire yield curve. *(See Figure C-7.)* Apparently, sustainable rents from fish harvests in the Gulf of Nicoya peaked in the early 1980s, according to these calculations.

Capitalizing the value of the annual sustainable rents at a discount rate of 6 percent yields the value of the Gulf's fishery asset. *(See Table C-7.)* The capital value depends not only on effort and its effect upon biomass and potential yields, but also on prices and costs. Therefore, each year the resource must be revalued for resource depreciation. This capital gain or loss due solely to price changes is not included in the estimated resource appreciation or depreciation. Instead, it is reported as a separate ''reval-

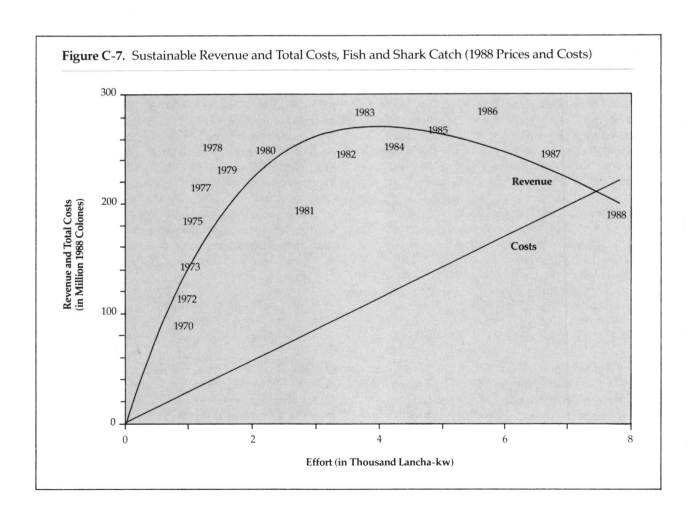

Figure C-7. Sustainable Revenue and Total Costs, Fish and Shark Catch (1988 Prices and Costs)

Table C-7. Value of Fishery Asset, Gulf of Nicoya

	Adjusted Effort (lancha-kw)	Annual Sustainable Rents (million 1984 colones)[a]	Asset Value (million 1984 colones)[b]
1970	1,009	65.7	1,095
1971	1,001	65.3	1,088
1972	991	65.1	1,086
1973	985	65.7	1,095
1974	993	66.8	1,114
1975	1,015	68.4	1,141
1976	1,060	70.0	1,167
1977	1,157	73.6	1,227
1978	1,352	79.3	1,321
1979	1,556	84.7	1,411
1980	2,208	90.5	1,509
1981	2,790	91.7	1,528
1982	3,431	82.0	1,366
1983	3,744	61.0	1,016
1984	4,238	59.4	990
1985	4,896	45.9	765
1986	5,683	33.9	565
1987	6,689	23.2	387
1988	7,831	−14.4	-240

a. Converted to 1984 colones using the wholesale price index.
b. Asset value *equals* the capitalized value of the annual rents. A 6 percent discount rate was used.

uation" column.[48] One year's depreciation, D_t, is calculated as one-year's change in asset value while effort increases but prices stay constant:

$$D_t = A(f_{t-1}, P_t) - A(f_t, P_t),$$

where, $A(f_t, P_t)$ is the asset value given the effort and price levels of year t. *(See Table C-8.)*

Resource Management Implications

The tables presented here indicate that the fisheries resource of the Gulf of Nicoya is being used far beyond its economic optimum. At the current level of exploitation, the economic value of the fishery is totally depleted, and artisanal fishermen are barely making sub-

The fisheries resource of the Gulf of Nicoya is being used far beyond its economic optimum. At the current level of exploitation, the economic value of the fishery is totally depleted, and artisanal fishermen are barely making subsistence incomes.

sistence incomes. The level of maximum sustainable rents was reached in the early 1980s,

Table C-8. Change in Value of Fishery Resource, Gulf of Nicoya (million 1984 colones)

Year	(A) Estimated Biomass[a] (tons)	(B) Opening Value	(C) Appreciation (depreciation)	(D) Closing Value[b]	(E) Revaluation $A(f_t, P_{t+1})$ less (D)
1970	4,931	—	—	1,095	(1)
1971	4,942	1,094	(6)	1,088	5
1972	4,954	1,093	(7)	1,086	14
1973	4,962	1,100	(5)	1,095	12
1974	4,951	1,107	6	1,114	10
1975	4,923	1,124	16	1,141	(6)
1976	4,867	1,134	33	1,167	(6)
1977	4,748	1,161	65	1,227	(17)
1978	4,517	1,210	112	1,321	(3)
1979	4,287	1,318	93	1,411	(40)
1980	3,628	1,371	138	1,509	26
1981	3,126	1,535	(6)	1,528	(63)
1982	2,653	1,465	(99)	1,366	(267)
1983	2,448	1,099	(83)	1,016	140
1984	2,157	1,156	(166)	990	48
1985	1,823	1,038	(273)	765	187
1986	1,490	951	(386)	565	384
1987	1,152	949	(562)	387	23
1988	860	409	(650)	(240)	—

— Not available.

a. Based on Eduardo Madrigal Abarca, "Dinámica pesquera de tres especies de sciaenidae corvinas en el Golfo de Nicoya, Costa Rica," Master of Science Thesis, Universidad de Costa Rica, Facultad de Biología, San José, Costa Rica, 1985, as discussed in the text.
b. Taken from Table C-7.

when fishing effort was less than 4,000 lancha-kw and the biomass was about 3 mt. Current effort levels are three times higher than in 1981, implying that a fishery-conservation program could actually increase fish production. In 1988, artisanal fishermen in the Gulf operated at a loss. If changes do not occur, fishermen's already low wages will soon be even lower.

Though not a substantial component of the national accounts, fishery depreciation is sectorially significant. If depreciation of the Gulf fishery is taken into account, gross fishery product grew during the 1980s at the expense of long-term productivity. (See Figure C-9.) Moreover, the gap between gross and net fishery product has widened. This assessment points to dramatically different conclusions about the management requirements for sustainable growth in Costa Rica's fisheries. Policies narrowly focused on current output will have to give way to resource-conservation strategies, balancing artisanal fishermen's need for employment with fishery sustainability.

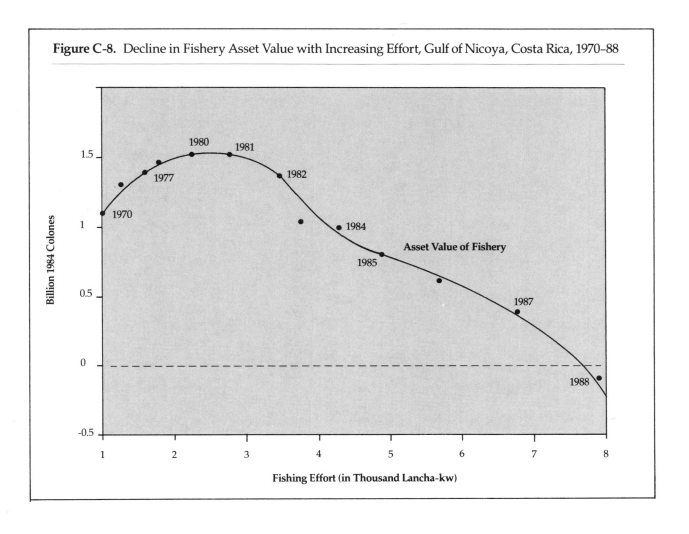

Figure C-8. Decline in Fishery Asset Value with Increasing Effort, Gulf of Nicoya, Costa Rica, 1970–88

Billion 1984 Colones

Fishing Effort (in Thousand Lancha-kw)

Asset Value of Fishery

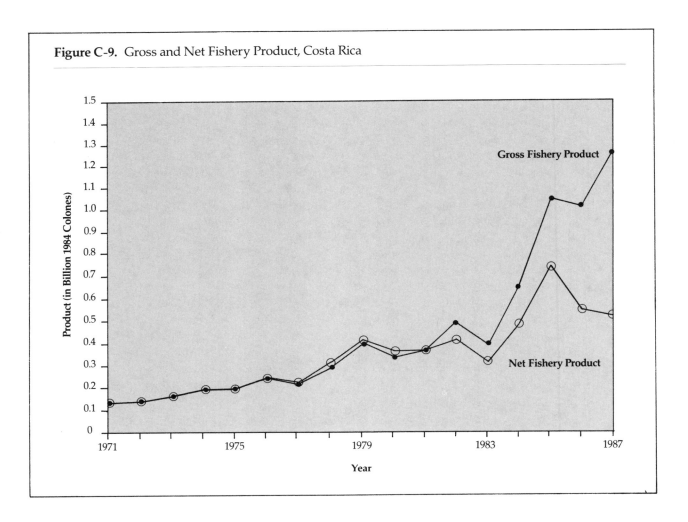

Figure C-9. Gross and Net Fishery Product, Costa Rica

D. Mangrove and Coastal Resource Accounts

Costa Rica has 1,200 km of coastline on the Pacific and 250 km along the Caribbean. *(See Figure D-1.)* Due to greater population density along the Pacific coast, natural resources there have been exploited more intensively than those on the Caribbean. The mangroves—one of the most important coastal resources—cover over 40,000 ha and extend over 35 percent of the Pacific coastline.

Because of severe deforestation on the coastal plain, mangroves are the only remaining forest cover in many areas. *(See Forestry Accounts,*

above). The highly productive forests provide local inhabitants with a great variety of primary and secondary products, directly and indirectly. The complex food chain linking the mangroves to the sea makes a great part of Costa Rican artisanal and semi-industrial fishing indirectly dependent on them. The dependent coastal species inhabiting the mangroves include *pianguas* and *chuchecas* (both known as mangrove cockles). Other dependent species inhabit the Gulf: *pargos* (snapper), *corvinas* (croaker), *lisas* (mullet), and many other commercial species.

High-quality charcoal is made from mangrove timber, and tannin is extracted from the bark. The ecosystem also provides coastal zones

Figure D-1. Gulf of Nicoya, Costa Rica

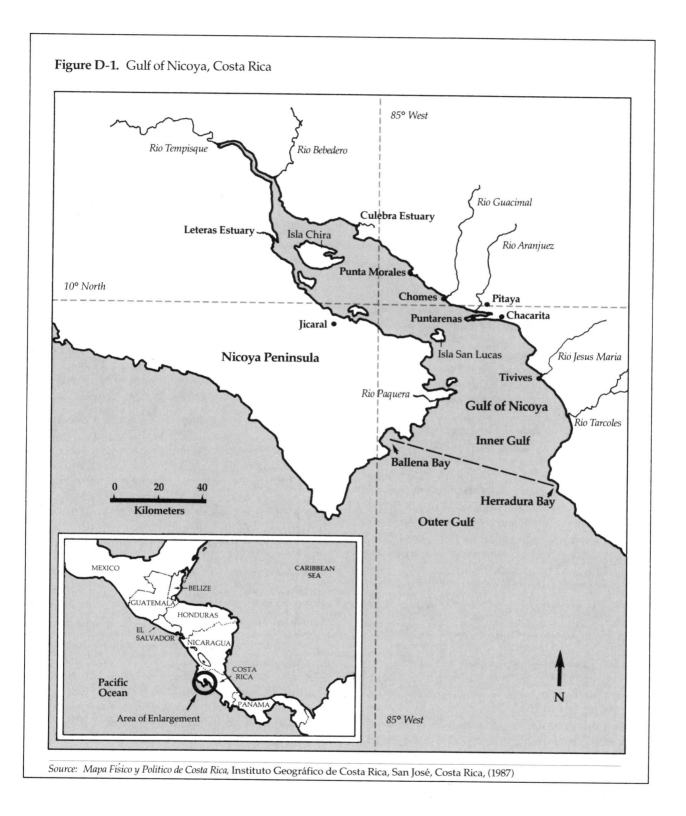

Source: *Mapa Físico y Político de Costa Rica,* Instituto Geográfico de Costa Rica, San José, Costa Rica, (1987)

with indirect economic benefits: wastewater oxidation, sediment retention, and erosion prevention.

Physical Accounts: Mangroves in Gulf of Nicoya

The Gulf of Nicoya (10° N, 85° W) is nearly 80 km long and 55 km wide at the mouth. For analysis, it is conventionally broken into inner and outer zones, divided by the strait between San Lucas Island and the Puntarenas Peninsula.

Rocks and cliffs, separated by sandy beaches, lie outside the Gulf. Except in a few small valleys along the river mouths (Jesus Maria, Tarcoles, Paquera), mangroves can't grow there.

Inside the Gulf, mangroves cover 112 km (42.6 percent) of the coastline. The inner Gulf is shallow, protected from the waves, and rich in lime-clay sediments favorable to mangroves.

Mangrove growth is intimately related to climate, precipitation levels, and proximity to fresh water. In wet zones, the forests are usually taller than those in drier climates.[49] The Gulf of Nicoya receives less than 1,800 mm of rain a year. As a result, tidal flooding is infrequent and light, and salt accumulates through evapotranspiration. Because of these conditions, the mangroves in the Gulf of Nicoya are relatively low. The genus *Rhizophora* and *Avicennia* predominate here.

The inner and outer sections of the Gulf of Nicoya also have different weather patterns. Precipitation in the inner section varies between 1,500 mm and 1,700 mm/yr, with a definite wet season between May and November and almost no rainfall the rest of the year. Here, large natural salt deposits left by evaporating seawater inhibit mangrove growth. Because of the rainfall pattern, the watersheds adjacent to these mangroves undergo seasonal ebbs and flows, especially on the Gulf's western rim. These fluctuations cause seasonal variations in soil salinity, which affects tree growth and reproduction. Most mangroves in this zone are stunted, and species that are adapted to high salinity predominate (Jiménez, 1990).

Similar conditions prevail over most of the Gulf's east coast except around the Puntarenas Peninsula and the Aranjuez, and Guacimal rivers, which drain higher rainfall areas. River flows in these areas fluctuate less than do those on the west coast. Mangroves surrounding these rivers are more highly developed, and salt flats are fewer.

In the outer Gulf, the climate is less severe, soil salinity less variable, and its flora are more diverse than in the inner Gulf. Rainfall varies between 1,800 mm and 3,000 mm/yr and is less seasonal. Tree height and basal area decline as distance from the nearest waterway increases. Drainage and run-off from nearby hills reduce salinity, but in dry weather salt flats form in the inner forest. A narrow band of *Avicennia* and *Laguncularia* usually grows around the salt flats.

The greatest dry mangrove diversity is observed deep inside forests, where high evaporation or fresh water infiltration can dramatically influence growing conditions. Where runoff and seasonal infiltration reduce drought and salinity, *Avicennia germinans* (L) is displaced by the less hardy *Avicennia bicolor Standl* (Jiménez, 1988a). Where soil salinity during the dry season is less than 50 p.p.m., strata of almost pure *Avicennia bicolor* grow with only an occasional *Avicennia germinans*. This pattern is inverted in places without runoff and infiltration.

Methodology

There are no reliable estimates of the mangrove area inside the Gulf of Nicoya, much less data on recent changes in cover. To fill in the missing information, aerial photos between coastlines of the inner Gulf were analyzed. For most zones, photos taken in 1965 and 1989 were used; for others, only photos for 1964 and 1979, or 1965 and 1985 were available. The mangroves were analyzed and mapped at a scale of 1:25,000. Each zone was subdivided into strata by composition (at genus level) and height. The changes in area and strata were calculated between 1964 and 1989. Because the zone was so large, field verification was done only around Tivives, Jicaral, Estero Pitahaya, and Punta Morales. To calculate changes in the strata volume, the estimates given in Table D-1 were used.[50]

Results

Current Surface Area. Mangroves cover 15,174 ha in the Gulf of Nicoya. Within this forest are 977 ha of artificial shrimp ponds and salt flats, and 584 ha of natural salt flats. This new estimate surpasses the previous 13,011 ha estimate by Jiménez (1990, p. 184).

As a result of the dry climate, medium tall *Rhizophora* and short *Avicennia* predominate in the Gulf mangroves. The salt ponds are concentrated around Jicaral, the Culebra Estuary, and Chomes. The current volume of the Gulf mangroves is 557,000 m³, concentrated primarily in *Rhizophora* strata. *(See Table D-2.)*

The largest expanses of mangroves are in the inner Gulf. The largest unbroken stretch of forest, 3,116 ha, lies between Chacarita and Punta Morales. The area also has 368 ha of ponds, concentrated around Chomes and used mainly for shrimp farming.

Historical Comparison. No significant changes in total forest cover occurred between 1964 and 1989. *(See Table D-3.)* Only 6.7 percent of the 1964 forest cover had disappeared in 1989 (1,066 ha). The two major causes of this reduction were the expansion in pond area (632 ha) and the conversion of mangroves and salt flats to agriculture and housing (349 ha).

The area under medium-sized *Avicennia* changed the most during the study period, declining by 1,854.55 ha (77,149.3 m³). Part of this reduction came from salt and shrimp pond construction, but most reflected the expansion of other species in mixed strata and of small *Avicennia*. These changes in composition and

Table D-1. Estimated Wood Volume from Different Strata, Gulf of Nicoya Mangroves

	Volume m³/ha[a]	Growth m³/ha/yr[b]
Rhizophora, tall	90.7	8
Rhizophora, medium	45.2	4
Rhizophora, low	8.9	2
Avicennia, tall	170	10
Avicennia, medium	41.6	5
Avicennia, low	7.0	3
Mixed tall	72.4	—
Mixed medium	39.8	—
Mixed low	10.4	—

— Unknown.

a. Based on J.A. Jiménez ''The Dynamics of *Rhizophora racemosa* Forests on the Pacific Coast of Costa Rica,'' *Brenesia* 30:1–2, 1988; J.A. Jiménez, ''The Structure and Function of Dry Weather Mangroves on the Pacific Coast of Central America, with Emphasis on *Avicennia bicolor* Forests,'' *Estuaries* 13 (2): 182–92, 1990; COHDEFOR, Corporación Hondureña de Desarrollo Forestal, ''Inventario Forestal Manglar del Sur, Golfo Fonseca,'' Report to United States Agency for International Development, AID/World Wildlife Fund/Asociación Hondureña de Ecología, Tegucigalpa, Honduras, 1987. (1988; 1990) and COHDEFOR in the Gulf of Fonseca (1987). The volumes are estimated for unmanaged mangroves.

b. Growth refers to the growth rates expected of managed mangroves.

height resulted from natural processes (such as progradation, rise in sea level, decrease of runoff) that affect each area differently. A net mangrove loss of 73,562 m³ is estimated, 11

Table D-2. Mangrove Area and Volume, Gulf of Nicoya, 1989

Strata	Area (ha)	Total Volume (m³)
Rhizophora, tall	1,478	134,059
Rhizophora, medium	4,052	183,156
Rhizophora, low	979	8,752
Avicennia, tall	354	60,170
Avicennia, medium	953	39,631
Avicennia, low	3,464	24,353
Mixed tall	214	15,513
Mixed medium	1,808	71,951
Mixed low	1,872	19,465
Subtotal, forest	15,174	557,050
Ponds	977	
Salt flats	583	
Total area	16,734	

The direct products of the forests include wood for lumber, telephone poles, fences, firewood, and charcoal. The bark of the *Rhizophora* genus (red mangrove) is harvested for its tannin, used in leather tanning.

Mangrove ecosystems can be exploited sustainably through stripcutting, natural and artificial regeneration, or rotations, thanks to the growth rates and volume levels common to these forests (Luna, 1976). If mangroves are not managed, however, the overextraction of products, particularly bark, can endanger the ecosystem (Morales, 1983).

So widely recognized is the mangrove's effectiveness in protecting the coastline that some countries plant them for that purpose (Linden and Jernelev, 1980). Mangrove cover also protects coastal inhabitants from tropical storms (Mercer and Hamilton, 1984).

Mangrove litter decomposition and transformation in detritus contribute directly to the marine food chain. The forest is a feeding ground for larva and juvenile shrimp such as the valuable *Peneidae*. The forest also serves as a refuge, feeding ground, and breeding ground for many other useful and rare species of flora and fauna (Mercer and Hamilton, 1984).

The mangrove ecosystems are suitable for raising fish, oysters, mussels, clams, shrimp, and other seafood. Salt can be extracted from ponds, making it possible to use them interchangeably for shrimp farming or salt production (Hamilton and Snedaker, 1984). Mangroves are good spots for fishing and hunting, and an important food and work resource for the coastal population (D'Croz and Kwiecinski, 1980). Because some species of the *Rhizophora*, *Avicennia*, *Laguncularia*, and *Conocarpus* genus provide pollen and nectar, many mangroves have potential for bee keeping and honey production (Hamilton and Snedaker, 1984).

Given mangroves' variety of habitats, uses, and species of flora and fauna, this ecosystem appears to have considerable potential as areas

percent of the 1964 volume. Heavy losses in *Avicennia* high and medium and *Rhizophora* tall stands were compensated by a 46-percent volume increase in mixed stands (33,650 m³).

From 1965 to 1989, the Gulf's mangrove area thus showed a simple variation of only 0.25 percent a year in ground cover and 0.46 percent in volume. Because this change is too slight to endanger the ecosystem, the annual change in mangrove area is not included in the economic accounts of the study.

Economic Value: Mangroves in Gulf of Nicoya

Review of the Literature

Mangroves supply the populace with a great variety of goods and services (Sánchez, 1986).

Table D-3. Change in Surface Area, Gulf of Nicoya Mangroves, 1964–89

Strata	Area (ha)		Difference
	1964	1989	
Rhizophora tall	1,696	1,478	−218
Rhizophora medium	3,911	4,052	141
Rhizophora low	1,260	979	−281
Avicennia tall	443	354	−89
Avicennia medium	2,807	953	−1,855
Avicennia low	3,334	3,464	130
Mixed tall	41	214	173
Mixed medium	1,408	1,808	400
Mixed low	1,369	1,872	502
Subtotal forest	16,269	15,174	−1,097
Ponds	344	977	632
Salt flats	468	583	115
Total area	17,081	16,734	347

Note: Some sections of this analysis were based on aerial photographs from 1979 and 1985.

for education, recreation, and tourism—all activities that can be compatible with ecosystem conservation (Hamilton and Snedaker, 1984). Despite this multitude of practical uses, however, only 1 percent of the world's mangroves are under legal protection (Hamilton and Snedaker, 1984). Mangroves urgently need more protection to preserve their genetic and economic wealth.

Direct Production

Mangrove Bark. Since pre-Columbian times, mangroves in the Gulf of Nicoya have been used for forest products, mainly tannins extracted from the *Rhizophora* bark. First used for seasoning nets, sails, and other fishing tools, tannin was later used for tanning leather (Meléndez, 1974). By the 1950s and 1960s, tannin extraction was the main economic activity in the mangroves, though it peaked in the

1970s. Only the Terraba Delta in the southern Pacific had more bark extraction concessions than did the Gulf of Nicoya (Morales, 1983, p. 13).

Morales (1983, p. 16) reported that 74 percent of the *Rhizophora* in the Letras Estuary had commercial value for tannin extraction. If this proportion of medium and tall strata of *Rhizophora* in the Gulf *(Table D-2)* is used to make an estimate, around 4,100 ha would support commercial exploitation of bark.

Mangrove management for bark cultivation should be based on 35-year cutting cycles for trees 25 cm or more in diameter, the minimum optimum cutting size (Jiménez, 1988b, p. 9). According to Morales (1983, p. 18), bark-yield estimates under this system vary from 1,840 kg/ha to 4,490 kg/ha and average 2,828 kg/ha. If calculations are based on this estimate, Gulf mangroves could sustainably yield up to 11.5 million kg of bark every 35 years, an average of 331 mt/yr.

Unprocessed bark is usually sold to intermediaries who transport the material to inland leather tanners. The costs of producing bark for on-site sale to intermediaries is presented in Table D-4. Improvements in basic technology for extracting tannins could significantly improve the price fetched per kilo of bark. In 1989, 1,260 kg of tannin were imported at a cost of US$1.3 million, an average of $1.04/kg (J. Valverde, COOPERCUR R.L., pers. com. 1990). In Costa Rica, tannins are extracted through an inefficient process in which bark is soaked in water. As a result, the price paid for bark is low, only $0.065/kg in 1989. Barely 5 percent of the tannins used by Costa Rica's industry come from domestic bark. Higher quality tannin from abroad has displaced the local product.

Charcoal. As bark exploitation has declined, charcoal production has steadily increased, particularly on the Gulf's eastern shore. Between Aranjuez and Chacarita, around 30 charcoal pits are in operation (Malavassi and associates, 1986, p. 12), but no production data are available.

Mangrove charcoal is an excellent fuel source, with nearly three-fourths the caloric content of fuel oil.[51] Most charcoal is consumed locally for domestic and some commercial uses. But, because technology permits charcoal to be substituted for fuel oil, international petroleum prices influence charcoal prices.

Information on charcoal costs and yields can be obtained for other parts of Costa Rica, but not for the Gulf of Nicoya. Chong (1988, p. 14) reported on the 21 charcoal pits operating in the Térraba area, which produce 1,230 m³ of charcoal annually. (*See Table D-5* for a summary of his findings on unit costs and incomes.)

Overall, the Gulf has 6,860 ha suitable for charcoal exploitation. This estimate includes all

Table D-4. Costs and Revenue from Mangrove Bark Exploitation, Gulf of Nicoya, 1983 (1983 colones/kg)

Production costs[a]	Value
Labor	2.95
Factor inputs	0.04
Transportation	0.53
Administration	0.40
Total	4.90
Unit price[b]	4.90
Profit	1.00

Source: Morales, 1983, Table 15.

a. Costs of harvesting and transporting the bark to an intermediary in the Gulf.
b. Price paid by intermediaries or tanners in the Gulf.

medium and tall strata of *Rhizophora* and *Avicennia*. The 35-year rotation cycle for *Rhizophora* bark implies the same cutting cycle for charcoal harvests. The *Avicennia* species, on the other hand, can be managed with a 25-year rotation for a sustainable harvest (Jiménez, 1988b, p. 9).

The total commercial volume of timber available for charcoal production in the Gulf is 285,500 m³ of *Rhizophora* and 89,800 m³ of *Avicennia*. If a conversion factor of 80 percent (Chong, 1988, p. 63) is assumed, 6,500 m³ of charcoal from *Rhizophora* and 2,900 m³ from *Avicennia* could be produced annually from the Gulf's mangroves.

Pianguas. Bivalve mollusk exploitation is common in the Gulf of Nicoya, especially *pianguas* (mangrove cockles, *Anadara tuberculosa* and *Anadara similis*). Archaeological discoveries have shown that indigenous communities based their diet on mangrove products and that the

Table D-5. Costs and Revenues from Charcoal Extraction in Costa Rica, 1988 (1988 US $/bag = 0.63 m³)

Extraction	0.19
Fuel	0.09
Transport[a]	0.07
Municipal taxes	0.07
Forest service taxes	0.13
Per diem and administrative costs	0.03
Subtotal, operating costs	0.58
Interest and depreciation[b]	0.07
Total costs	0.65
Price of final product	0.87
Net income	0.22

Note: Approximations based on Chong (1988), assuming that 90 percent of the production is commercialized.

Source: P.W. Chong, Forest Management Plan for Playa Garza Pilot Area: Terraba-Sierpe Mangrove Reserve, Report prepared for the Government of Costa Rica by the Food and Agriculture Organization of the United Nations (FAO), San José, Costa Rica. FAO-DGF [Dirección General Forestal] Technical Report 3, July 1988.

a. Transport to highway or collection point.
b. Corresponds to the investment in boats and motors with a unit value of US $1,000.

average mollusk harvested today is smaller than those consumed by the pre-Columbian Indians.[52]

Pianguas grow in low and medium strata (ñangas) of *Rhizophora* and are thus exposed to periodic tidal flooding. According to estimates derived from the Térraba mangroves, *pianguas* occur in these strata in a density of $1.5/m^2$ (J. Campos, pers. com., 1990). If *pianguas* occur at this density in half of the Gulf's medium and low *Rhizophora* (5,030 ha.), its total *pianguas* population can be estimated at 37.7 million.

According to estimates by the Fishing Communities Training Program at the National University (PCCP-UNA, 1987, p. 5) *piangua* gatherers harvest these mollusks year round. Approximately 150 gatherers work the Gulf of Nicoya alone. Each gatherer extracts 200 to 300 mollusks daily, four to five days a week. Collection costs are minimal because the mollusks need only be picked up from the mangrove floor.

The Gulf mangrove harvest is estimated at 8 million *pianguas*/yr. Gatherers sell the mollusks for 2.25 colones apiece to the collection center, for resale at 3 colones apiece. Based on these estimates, 21 percent of the Gulf's *pianguas* stock is harvested annually. Because the effects of this harvest rate on stocks are unknown, no limits can be set for maximum sustainable yield (MSY). Pending further study, it is estimated, for the purposes of this study, that a 15-percent harvest level would be below MSY and would permit *piangua* production to be sustained.

Pollution from urban wastewater has contaminated the beds near the city of Puntarenas with chloroform. This type of contamination could spread to *piangua* beds elsewhere, jeopardizing their economic value.

Shrimp. Aquaculture in ponds within Gulf mangroves has developed rapidly. Semi-intensive shrimp farms and small artisanal operations are common. The semi-intensive activities do not impinge on mangroves since the farms are located on their inner edges. Artisanal shrimp farms lack pumps and depend upon nature for their constant supply of water. These ponds operate in abandoned salt flats, though their expansion would require further conversion of the region's mangroves.

Kapetsky and associates (1987, p. 27) reported that 2,232 ha adjacent to the Gulf mangroves could be converted to sites for semi-intensive shrimp farming. (This estimate is based on the availability of fresh water and suitable soils.) Most areas with this potential lie along the northern rim of the Gulf, and 977 ha are already being used in semi-intensive and artisanal ponds.

Semi-intensive shrimp farming in the Gulf of Nicoya is carried out in two or more annual cycles, yielding 900 kg to 1,200 kg of shrimp/yr/ha. Pond-construction costs on this kind of farm are nearly US$5,000/ha (CAAP, 1987, p. 136), and such ponds have a useful life of seven years. Daily production costs on semi-intensive farms amount to $11/day/ha (F. Vivez, Maricultura Chomes, S.A., pers. com, 1990).[53]

Artisanal shrimp operations use less intensive production systems in smaller ponds, usually on abandoned salt flats. Establishing this type of production costs only $3,600/ha (CAAP, 1987, p. 136). Operating costs are minimal since pumped water is not used and the owner usually does the work.

Nearly a quarter (150 ha) of the Gulf's salt flats could be turned into artisanal shrimp ponds (Kapetsky and associates, 1987, p. 27). The annual yields in artisanal operations are variable, but average about 600 kg/ha (Dickinson and associates 1985). The *Pneus vnamei* shrimp cultivated in these ponds are harvested in two main sizes, 21 to 25 tails/kg, priced at US$5.5/kg, and 41 to 50 tails/kg for $3/kg, in the ratio 60 percent and 40 percent, respectively.

Indirect Production

All mangroves provide a variety of other products and services, most of them unquantifiable for lack of information. The mangroves' role in Gulf shrimp fishing and in protecting birds (see below) are examples. Also important, though not discussed here, is the mangroves' wastewater-purification function.

Role in Shrimp Breeding Cycle. The interdependence between fisheries and coastal vege-

tation has been recognized for some time (Turner, 1977). *Peneidos* shrimp, for example, hatch in the mangroves. The maximum sustainable yield of the *peneidos* fisheries is related to the surface area of the coastal vegetation (Turner, 1977). Pauly and Ingles (1986) correlated the maximum sustainable yield (MSY) of *peneidos* with intertidal vegetation cover (int. veg.) and latitude (lat) using the function:

$$\log_{10}(\text{MSY}) = 2.41 + 0.4875 \cdot \log_{10}(\text{int. veg.}) - 0.0212 \cdot \text{degrees lat.}$$

The function infers, therefore, that the Gulf of Nicoya, with a total mangrove area of 15,173 ha and an average latitude of 10°N, should have an MSY of 1,933 mt/yr. Shrimp catches are reported in terms of tails sold. An estimated 61.4 percent of the catch by weight is composed of tails (NORAD/FAO/OLDEPESCA p. 116). The maximum sustainable catch therefore should be approximately 1,187 mt/yr. Of course, such estimates must be interpreted very cautiously.

The values presented in Table D-6 indicate that actual harvest levels are close to the maximum sustainable level. Harvests in 1985 through 1987 exceeded the estimated MSY rate probably because climatic conditions known as *El Niño* diminished yields in 1983 and 1984 and caused bumper harvests in the following period (E. Madrigal, DGRP, pers. com., 1991).

Finally, the cost to shrimp fishing from mangrove loss can be inferred. Applying the formula directly to the loss of one hectare of mangrove would imply a 62 kg/yr drop in MSY. Although the relationship is not that simple, all evidence indicates that large losses of mangrove would substantially damage shrimp fishing in the Gulf.

Bird Sanctuary. The Gulf of Nicoya mangroves also have an unquantified value as a refuge and migratory stop-over for birds. Hernandez (pers. com., 1985) counted 65 species of birds, 7 of them rare or in danger of extinction. Another 19 species peculiar to the man-

Table D-6. Gulf Shrimp Harvests, 1970–88

Year	Shrimp Harvest by Type (mt)					Total	% of Estimated MSY
	White	Pink	Brown	Small	Fidel		
1970	120	51	0	597	27	795	67.0%
1971	168	59	1	779	1	1,007	84.9%
1972	120	24	0	636	9	790	66.5%
1973	135	30	0	671	2	838	70.6%
1974	102	105	1	621	12	841	70.9%
1975	93	87	3	611	15	808	68.1%
1976	137	86	7	544	10	784	66.1%
1977	78	38	5	244	11	376	31.7%
1978	54	28	2	278	8	371	31.3%
1979	105	63	1	414	43	626	52.8%
1980	198	53	1	286	57	595	50.1%
1981	233	52	1	304	71	660	55.6%
1982	153	74	2	331	258	818	68.9%
1983	56	61	5	212	108	442	37.3%
1984	140	186	10	389	187	913	76.9%
1985	372	198	7	346	1,128	2,051	172.8%
1986	150[a]	39	2	200	638	1,309	110.3%
1987	261[a]	67	1	311	169	1,230	103.6%
1988	135	99	3	483	66	786	66.2%

Note: Mangrove area based in metric tons.

Source: Dirección de Recursos Pesqueros y Acuacultura, unpublished data.

a. The sums of the columns do not coincide with the established harvest in the years 1986 and 1987, when the total harvests were increased by 280 mt and 420 mt respectively, to account for harvests by artisanal fishermen not disaggregated in the data.

grove depend on its ecosystem, and 17 migratory birds (most of them native to North America) spend part of the year in the mangroves and need the ecosystem to maintain the species.

Economic Potential: Mangroves in Gulf of Nicoya

Mapping for this study showed that the mangroves in the Gulf of Nicoya have not lost much surface area (only 1,096 ha in 25 years).

The forest may have suffered some degradation due to charcoal exploitation and debarking for tannin, but the extent of the losses is unknown. Analysis of mangrove change between 1961 and 1989 has permitted changes in total surface area and composition to be determined, but not changes in the genetic composition of the biomass.

The mangroves represent resources that could be economically important regionally. A hypothetical mangrove management system was analyzed for the following benefits:

- charcoal production from tall and medium *Rhizophora, Avicennia.* The rotation period for charcoal from *Rhizophora* was estimated at 35 years; for *Avicennia,* 25 years.

- bark stripping for tannin. This is possible only with *Rhizophora,* with a rotation cycle of 35 years.

- *pianguas* production for the national market. Pianguas are assumed to occur at an average rate of 1.5 individuals per m² in 50 percent of the *Rhizophora* mangroves. (J. Campos, pers. com., 1990). A harvest of 15 percent of the population annually is considered sustainable.

- semi-intensive shrimp production at the edge of the mangrove and on solid land. Some 2,232 ha would be suitable for semi-intensive shrimp farming.

The unit values used in the analysis are presented in Table D-7. They were converted from values for several years into 1989 values, using the wholesale price index. The real interest rate used in the analysis is 6 percent.

Many other values directly attributable to mangroves have not been evaluated here. Among these are mangroves' role in protecting biodiversity, purifying wastewater, and sheltering migratory birds. Although currently unquantifiable, these values should be considered in developing optimum-use plans, and conversion to other uses (i.e., agriculture or shrimp farms) should not be considered without much further study.

In summary, the mangrove system has a total of 17,406 ha: 6,509 ha are suitable for *pianguas* harvesting; 5,530 ha for bark exploitation; 6,837 ha for charcoal production; and 2,232 ha for shrimp farming. Another 3,892 ha of mixed mangrove deserves protection because of its indirect role in maintaining the system.

Table D-8 shows the present values of the management plan components and the total systemic value. After the 6-percent normal return on capital is taken into account, the system rent inferred by the model is low, and the present value of the benefits exceeds costs by only 0.3 percent. The value of the system, however, would be at least 12 million colones greater if mangroves were managed.

The calculations show that sustainably managed mangroves could contribute sizeable benefits, at least regionally. Any increase in production would be valuable in Guanacaste and Puntarenas provinces, where unemployment exceeds the national average (9.2 percent and 10.7 percent, respectively, compared to the 6.2 percent nationally (DG Estadística y Censos, 1987b).

Table D-7. Summary of Values Used to Calculate Worth of Gulf Mangroves' Direct Products (1989 colones)

	No./yr	Unit cost		No./yr	Unit cost
General costs/yr			Municipal taxes	—	79.4
Silviculture, days/ha cut	6	518	DGF taxes	—	158.7
Technicians	3	750,000	Administration and		
Engineers	6	450,000	per diem	—	36.2
Protection, 0.5 days/ha/yr	—	518	Total variable cost/m³	—	753.3
Investments, useful life 4 yr			Investments, every 5 yrs	—	4,273,846
Boats	15	1,223,700	Revenue/m³, Rhizophora		
Trucks	4	522,112	charcoal	—	1,049.9
			Revenue/m³, Avicennia		
Bark			charcoal	—	892.4
Annual Production (kg)	330,661	—			
Operating costs/kg			**Pianguas**		
Labor	—	5.30	Annual harvest/thousand		
Supplies	—	0.07	pianguas	5,660	—
Transport	—	0.93	Labor, days	2,640	518
Total variable cost/kg	—	6.31	Revenue/thousand		
Revenue/kg	—	8.81	pianguas	—	2,250
Charcoal			**Shrimp**		
Annual production (m³),			Yield/ha/yr (kg)	1,000	—
Rhizophora	6,525	—	Total area (ha)	2,232	—
Annual production (m³),			Construction cost/ha/7 yrs		
Avicennia	2,874	—	(70% Value Added)	—	407,900
Operating costs/m³	—	—	Operating costs/ha/day		
Extraction	—	269.87	(80% Valued Added)	260	897
Fuel	—	113.1	Average revenue/kg	—	367
Transport	—	96.1			

— Not applicable.

Table D-8. Summary: Management System for Direct Products, Gulf Mangroves (thousand 1989 colones)

	Component Totals	System Totals
Present Value of One 35-year Rotation		
Income, forestry/piangua component	388,993	
Income, shrimp component	12,182,799	
Income, complete system		12,571,792
Factor inputs, forestry/piangua component	50,444	
Factor inputs, shrimp component	2,422,877	
Factor inputs, system		2,473,320
Total expenses, forestry/piangua component	338,368	
Total expenses, shrimp component	10,896,639	
Total expenses, general	153,879	
Total expenses, complete system		11,388,885
Administration, forestry/piangua component	33,837	
Administration, shrimp component	1,089,664	
Administration, general	15,388	
Administration, complete system		1,138,889
Value Added, forestry/piangua component[a]	338,550	
Value Added, shrimp component[a]	9,759,922	
Value Added, system		10,098,472
Rent, forestry/piangua component[a]	11,367	
Rent, shrimp component[a]	32,652	
Rent, complete system		44,019
Present Value, Sustainable Mangrove Use[b]		
Soil expectation value, system		50,602
Present value of value added		11,608,843
Rent/ha, mangrove		3.3
Rent/ha, system		2.9
Value added/ha		667.0
Average Values/Year		
Rent/ha/yr		2.5
Value added/ha/yr		39.0

a. Administrative expenses are distributed between the forestry/pianguas and shrimp in the same proportion as annual incomes.
b. Assumes an infinite number of 35-yr rotations.

Wilfrido Cruz is an environmental economist at The World Bank. Formerly, he was a resource economist in WRI's Economics, Technology, and Institutions program. Dr. Cruz specializes in forest resource management, soil erosion valuation, and coastal fishery assessment. He has undertaken numerous resource policy studies in developing countries in Asia and Latin America.

Ronnie de Camino is director of the sustainable development project at the Deutsche Gesell Schaft Für Technische Zusammenarbeit (GTZ) in Costa Rica. Formerly, he was the regional coordinator for the Central American Tree Crops Production Project (MADELEÑA) at the Centro Agronómico Tropical de Investigación y Enseñanza (CATIE) in Turrialba, Costa Rica.

Jorge Jiménez is vice-president of The Tropical Science Center. He conducts research on mangrove and coastal resource management at the National University of Costa Rica, where he is a member of the University Advisory Council.

Robert Repetto is Chief Economist and Director of the Program in Economics, Technology, and Institutions at the World Resources Institute. Formerly, he was an associate professor of economics at the School of Public Health at Harvard University and a member of the economics faculty at Harvard's Center for Population Studies.

Raúl Solórzano is executive director of the Tropical Science Center. Formerly director of the National Program of Renewable Natural Resources (CORENA), Mr. Solórzano is a professor of agronomy at the University of Costa Rica and professor of forestry administration at the National University in Costa Rica.

Joseph Tosi is president of the Tropical Science Center where he has worked for thirty years. One of his best-known studies is the methodology of universal application to determine land use capacity based on the world life zones system by Dr. L.R. Holdridge. He is presently working on the study of the effect of climate change on ecology and land use capacity.

Alexis Vásquez is the former General Director of Investigation and Agricultural Extension at the Ministry of Agriculture. Mr. Vásquez has worked as a consultant for numerous organizations including The Food and Agriculture Organization, the World Bank, and the Centro Agronómico Tropical de Investigacíon y Enseñanza (CATIE).

Carlos Villalobos is a professor and researcher at The University of Costa Rica, School of Biology. He was scientific advisor to the President of Costa Rica from 1978 through 1982 in the area of marine sciences.

Vicente Watson is an associate consultant to the Tropical Science Center in applied ecological work including: classifying and mapping land use, mapping of life zones, forestry inventories, and reforestation plans.

Richard Woodward is presently a graduate student at the University of Wisconsin. He assisted the authors of WRI's *Wasting Assets*, a natural resources accounting study on Indonesia and lived in Costa Rica for the duration of the present study.

Annexes

Annex A-1
Calculating Timber Volumes

To correlate the physical qualities of the land units with their probable vegetation and original volume, the following procedure was used:

• **First step.** The results of a study of Costa Rica's primary natural forests and related physical environments between 1964 and 1966 (Holdridge and associates, 1971) were used as the primary, though not exclusive, empirical base for the analysis. This study examined in detail the natural primary vegetation, lithology, geomorphology, and soils corresponding to 44 original vegetative associations distributed in 10 different life zones throughout the country. Each study site was located on the land unit map, and the land unit or units corresponding directly to each association was precisely determined.

• **Second step.** Analogous and near-analogous land units were found by combining similar slope characteristics and similar categories of soil parent material, life zones, and soils subgroups. For those land units not represented in or analogous to those in the system developed by Holdridge and associates (1971), values of the available data were extrapolated and reference was made to other studies, such as Swedforest AB (1977) and TSC (1987). Finally, 45 class-groupings for all 860 discrete land units were obtained.

• **Third step.** For each reference plant association, mean annual evapotranspiration (ETR) was estimated in millimeters of precipitation equivalents (m.p.e.), according to the formula (Holdridge, 1967 pp. 102–104):

$$ETR = 29.47 \cdot \text{height} \cdot \frac{\text{no. of actual strata}}{\text{no. of strata in climatic association}}$$
$$(\text{in m})$$

• **Fourth step.** The net annual above-ground primary productivity in tons of dry matter per ha was calculated employing the formula proposed by Tosi (1980a, pp. 44–64), following Rosenzweig (1968) and Holdridge (1967):

$$NPP = ETR \cdot 0.027.$$

• **Fifth step.** With reference to Holdridge and associates (1971), each association and, by extension, each land unit was characterized according to the following criteria.

A = number of species present in the association
B = number of species per 0.1 ha
C = number of trees in a 0.1 ha plot > 9.9 cm. d.b.h. (diameter at breast height)
D = average height of superior canopy (in m)
E = basal area (in m²/0.1 ha) of all trees > 9.9 cm d.b.h.

F = average height of trunk between minimum stump and first live branch (in m)

• **Sixth Step.** Potential timber volume (G) (in m³/ha) was estimated for round timber with diameters greater than 9.9 cm, by the formula:

$$G = \text{Trunk volume} = (F) \cdot (E) \cdot 0.67 \cdot 10.$$

The average volume was estimated as 80% of the potential (G).

• **Seventh step.** To distribute the round timber into hard, medium, and soft woods, the total volume per ha (G) was *multiplied* by the percentage distribution of the species present in each density class by volume. This calculation was based on density measurements, using specific gravities of species present in the same associations and in other forests, characterized by life zone in Costa Rica and Brazil (Chudnoff, 1974).

Type	Density	Estimated average
Soft	≤ 0.39	0.30
Medium	0.40 − 0.59	0.50
Hard	≥ 0.60	0.80.

• **Eighth Step.** The average density of timbers in each association (H) was calculated by *multiplying* the averages estimated for the hard, medium, and soft wood classes by the volumes in each class, and dividing the sum by the total volume of each association.

• **Ninth step.** The annual potential volume increment of all species under intensive natural forest management, MAI, (I) in m³ of round timber per year between the stump and the first live branch of trees greater than 9.9 cm. d.b.h. was estimated on the basis of the formula:

$$I = \frac{NPP \times 0.64}{H} \cdot \frac{F}{D}$$

An estimated 90 percent of net primary productivity consists of stems and live branches, including bark (timber). To compensate for the remaining 10 percent and trunk defects, the calculated volume was reduced by 20 percent.

The unadjusted results indicate only the potential volume by biotype under intensive professional management, starting from natural mature forest. This volume in round timber could theoretically be transformed into various products, including fuelwood, in a hypothetical economy that maximizes long-term sustainable production from all forest resources. Because maximum biological productivity differs from maximum economic productivity, average growth was estimated at 80 percent of potential (yielding the 0.64 adjustment factor in the last equation). *(See Table A-1-1.)*

These volume and growth estimates are much higher than those obtained using conventional forest inventories and experimental growth plots in mature natural unmanaged forests. The following points must, however, be kept in mind.

• These data are based on exact detailed measurements with precision instruments for each tree in plots of 1/10 ha, measured and marked on the site, with several replications in each association studied. The site level results were then adjusted downward by a factor of 0.64 to conservatively estimate the average timber volume in each ecological association. In contrast, forest inventory measurements are generally quick and crude estimates, made with poor instruments or without instruments.

• The basal area includes all the rigid trunk species with d.b.h. of 10 cm and more, without exception. In other words, it includes the palms but not the lianas. In commercial inventories, only the species considered "commercial" (generally a subjective criteria) are taken into account. The minimum diameter considered is usually 40 cm, not 10 cm.

• The total volume of round timber (as estimated in the present study) is not comparable to the volume determined by traditional forest inventories. Here volume was determined based upon the raw data obtained by the above mentioned measurements with corrections made subsequently for the taper, bark, morphic form and possible defects. This volume is a more exact estimate of round timber volume for each type of forest since it includes total woody biomass useful in some types of products not generally considered, such as fuelwood. It is not and it does not pretend to be the ''commercial'' volume of sawn wood.

Table A-1-1. Land Unit Characteristics by Life Zone

| Site #[a] | Ecological Association[a] | Total Stand Height (m) | Number of Trees/ha | Timber Volume (m³/ha) | | | | |
				Mean Annual Increment	Hard Wood	Semi-Hard Wood	Soft Wood	%> 50 cm[b]
Tropical Dry Forest and Premontane Moist Forest Transition to Basal Belt
1A	NC	22	580	2.0	18	13	16	38
1B	WE/IE	29	350	5.5	78	50	66	44
1C	DE	7	78	<0.1	<1	<1	<1	0
1D	DE	9	470	0.3	4	4	3	0
1E	WE	24	335	1.7	3	18	54	42
1F	WE	33	167	5.6	51	102	34	27
1G	FE	44	265	13.6	72	202	66	68
Tropical Moist Forest
2A	DA	45	506	11.9	159	159	54	40
2B	DA	43	353	12.1	92	186	62	62
2C	DA/DE	30	500	6.5	51	114	26	34
3	FE	40	590	12.9	94	212	47	84
20A	NC	39	540	10.6	208	134	60	50
20D	DE	30	590	8.0	135	106	25	44
23	DE	30	550	8.5	169	13	60	40
Tropical Wet Forest
4	WE	43	600	18.6	98	266	111	57
8A	C	54	520	20.3	209	228	104	50
8B	VWE	26	235	1.3	88	2	2	68
8C	H/IE	34	360	1.8	81	0	0	0
8D1	WE/FE	0	540	14.9	191	261	131	61
8D2	FE	48	240	20.4	178	357	179	75
8E	WE/IE	5	420	16.7	113	165	35	58
8F	DE	36	690	15.5	174	227	112	49
19A	WA	43	510	17.3	217	262	142	60
19B	WA/IE	0	520	10.2	55	91	36	48
19C	WA/VWE/FE	47	290	11.2	0	678	0	87
19E	WA/VWE	40	720	9.1	277	434	78	25
19F	WA	40	440	14.5	138	180	86	52
Premontane Moist Forest
18	NC	23	490	5.5	45	52	26	52
21	NC	22	570	5.7	126	12	22	41

Table A-1-1. (Continued)

Site #[a]	Ecological Association[a]	Total Stand Height (m)	Number of Trees/ha	Timber Volume (m³/ha) Mean Annual Increment	Hard Wood	Semi-Hard Wood	Soft Wood	%> 50 cm[b]
				Premontane Wet Forest				
7	IE	44	500	13.8	100	105	47	39
11	WA	46	410	17.8	160	270	122	
15A	DA/IE	38	580	7.1	92	84	28	18
15B	DA/IE	32	630	13.5	104	119	59	25
15C	DA/IE	29	570	11.4	69	74	31	37
16	FE	34	440	11.6	189	146	58	52
				Premontane Rain Forest				
5	DE	42	580	13.1	100	70	29	30
22A	NC	42	636	11.9	74	113	44	44
22B	WE	39	640	10.7	70	115	30	25
22D	FE	46	540	15.2	150	248	65	40
22E	WA	38	700	11.4	81	142	22	25
				Lower Montane Moist Forest				
17	DE	33	400	8.3	184	70	27	44
				Lower Montane Wet Forest				
10	FE/DA	23	520	6.1	102	107	46	44
				Lower Montane Rain Forest				
9A	NC	27	500	5.3	110	42	15	46
9B	FE/DE	49	430	12.8	691	38	41	46
12	WA/DE	20	940	3.8	105	117	11	33
				Montane Rain Forest				
6	NC	30	610	3.5	210	32	20	34

Note: Land units are ecological associations by life zone, as in L.R. Holdridge, *Life Zone Ecology* (San José, Costa Rica: Tropical Science Center), 1967. C = climatic; NC = near climatic; WE = wet edaphic; VWE = very wet edaphic; DE = dry edaphic; IE = infertile edaphic; FE = fertile edaphic; DA = dry atmospheric; WA = wet atmospheric; H = hydric.

a. L.R. Holdridge; W.C. Grenke, W.H. Hathaway, T. Liang, J.A. Tosi, *Forest Environments in Tropical Life Zones: A Pilot Study,*(Oxford, New York, Toronto, Sydney, Braunschweig: Pergamon Press), 1971.
b. Percentage of the volume in logs with diameters greater than 50 cm.

Annex A-2
Tropical Forest Volumes and Growth Rates

Source	Volume (m³/ha)	Diameter Range (cm)	Mean Annual Increment (m³/ha/yr)	Location	Observations
TSC, 1987	186	+25	6.5	Costa Rica	Primary humid forest
Blaser, 1987	423–562	+50	—	Costa Rica	Cloud forest
Herrera, 1990	110–359	+10	5.4–8.9	Costa Rica	Secondary forest 17-to-40 yr-old
Marmillod, 1982	46–286	+10	—	Peru	Amazon forest
Sabogal, 1987	399	+10	—	Peru	Amazon forest
Heheisel, 1976	99–819	+10	—	Venezuela	Cloud forest
Bockor, 1977	392	+10	—	Venezuela	Cloud forest
	575	+10	—	Venezuela	Podocarpus forest
Malleux, 1982	71–121	+40	—	Peru	Alluvial forest
UNESCO/UNEP, FAO, 1980	188–796	—	4.8–20	General	—
Brown & Lugo, 1990	—	—	27.5–33.8	Costa Rica	Secondary forest[a]

— Not available.

a. Brown and Lugo cite Rosero who measured secondary forest.

Annex A-3
Indexes Used in Calculating ET&M Costs

Year	Fuel Price Index	Exchange Rate c/$	General Wholesale P-Index	Minimum Wage Index	Cost of Electricity colones/kw
1970	0.02	6.64	0.05	0.08	0.09
1971	0.03	6.64	0.06	0.09	0.09
1972	0.03	6.64	0.06	0.09	0.10
1973	0.03	6.65	0.07	0.10	0.10
1974	0.06	7.96	0.10	0.12	0.15
1975	0.07	8.57	0.12	0.14	0.20
1976	0.07	8.57	0.13	0.16	0.24
1977	0.07	8.57	0.14	0.17	0.28
1978	0.07	8.57	0.15	0.20	0.29
1979	0.11	8.57	0.17	0.22	0.30
1980	0.38	8.57	0.21	0.26	0.34
1981	0.72	21.76	0.35	0.32	0.48
1982	1.00	37.41	0.74	0.56	0.81
1983	1.00	41.09	0.93	0.85	1.46
1984	1.00	44.53	1.00	1.00	1.61
1985	1.00	50.45	1.10	1.20	1.88
1986	1.01	55.99	1.20	1.37	2.03
1987	1.03	62.81	1.33	1.54	2.23
1988	1.12	75.89	1.57	1.76	2.76
1989	1.14	81.58	1.80	2.11	3.32

Source: Banco Central de Costa Rica, Sección de Cuentas Nacionales.

Annex A-4
Calculating Stumpage Value and Capital Value

Stumpage value is expressed mathematically as:

(1) $SV = P_s - (1+i) \cdot (C_I + C_T + C_H)$,

where:

SV	=	stumpage value,
P_s	=	price of marketable products,
i	=	standard profit margin or return on capital, equal to the prevailing interest rate,
C_I	=	cost of industrialization or milling,
C_T	=	cost of transport, and
C_H	=	harvesting costs.

All values are first expressed as monetary units (colones, ¢) per cubic meter of round wood equivalent (RWE). For example, suppose that a tree with 17 m³ of total volume produces 10 m³ of logs that can be processed into 5 m³ of sawn wood. If the price of sawnwood is ¢100/m³, and the total cost to extract and convert the standing wood into sawnwood is ¢400, including the cost of the capital, then the stumpage value for this tree is ¢100, ¢10/m³ RWE. The value per m³ RWE is finally converted into value per m³ of total forest volume—in this case, yielding a unit value of ¢5.9/m³ of forest volume.

The *capital value* of an irregular forest managed sustainably can be determined mathematically as an extension of the Faustmann formula of soil expectation value (Gregory, 1976):

$$(2) \quad V_{SM} = CVO_1 \cdot SV + \frac{MAI \cdot cc \cdot SV - \Sigma\, C_j\, (1+i)^{(cc-j)}}{(1+i)^{cc} - 1},$$

where:

V_{SM}	=	value of forest under sustainable management,
CVO_1	=	marketable volume cut in first year of intervention,
SV	=	stumpage value in year of harvest, which also equals stumpage value at time of future harvests if prices are constant,
MAI	=	mean annual increment under intensive management,
cc	=	cutting cycle in years,
C_j	=	costs of forestry management in year j of the cutting cycle
i	=	interest rate.

This formula implies that cycles start with a timber harvest and are repeated indefinitely. The formula represents the potential timber value of a natural forest. When a forest is cleared, national forest assets are decreased by depleting both standing commercial timber and future harvests of valuable wood.

Annex A-5
Value of Secondary Forests, by Volume
(1989 colones)

	Total
Costs	
Operating costs/ha	34,106
Forest fund taxes	21,427
Total costs	55,533
Revenues	
Firewood, 90 m³	38,841
Timber, 136 m³	353,099
Total revenue	391,940
Net revenue (rent)	336,407
Standing value/m³	1,488

Source: R. Herrera. Evaluación financiera del manejo del bosque natural secundario en 5 sitios en Costa Rica. Master's Thesis, CATIE (Centro Agronómico Tropical de Investigación y Enseñanza), Turialba, Costa Rica, 1990, Table 4a.

Annex B-1
Soil Depreciation and Productivity Loss

Nutrient loss estimates though easily understood, do not fully reflect the economic costs of soil erosion. As soil erodes, the direct economic effect comes from declining agricultural productivity. Lal (1985, p. 333) points out:

[In] some tropical soils...erosion cannot be compensated for through the application of fertilizer. For this reason, the value of the nutrients washed away is not a complete measure of the economic depreciation of the soil.

Nonetheless, estimating the relationship between erosion and productivity is difficult because empirical studies are lacking and because tropical soils are so diverse. Lal (1987, p. 333) mentions studies in Nigeria (Mbagwu and associates, 1984, and Lal, 1985), Cameroon (Rehm, 1978), Malaysia (Siew and Fatt, 1976), and Hawaii (Yost and associates 1985) that show that the loss of a few centimeters of the upper soil layers notably reduced soil fertility. However, the diversity of conditions, practices, and crops virtually precludes extrapolation of study results from one country or region to another with any precision. Because the nutrient loss method is not entirely satisfactory, direct estimates of productivity losses have been made for selected crops and soil types to provide a partial cross-check.

The EPIC Model

In reaction to the Resource Conservation Act in the United States, Williams and Renard (1985) developed the Erosion Productivity Index Calculator (EPIC) to analyze erosion, plant growth, and their economic implications. EPIC uses a linear program model and a data base of thousands of observations on climate, soil, management practices, and crops. The model mathematically generates daily climate for a site and then simulates crop growth and annual erosion.

Though developed in the United States for temperate soils, the model can use data developed for any site. Nonetheless, variables that affect the productivity of tropical soils, such as microbacterial action and compaction, are not incorporated in the model (A. Jones, Agricultural Experiment Station, Temple, Texas, pers. com., 1990). In Costa Rica, the data necessary to use EPIC are available for few sites. Because nationwide analysis with EPIC would be impossible, the model was used to compare the estimates of depreciation at four sites under three traditional crops with those derived by the nutrient loss approach. The model was adjusted for Costa Rican conditions and crops with help from the Agricultural Experiment Station in Temple, Texas.

Methodology and Results

The main characteristics of the sites chosen for analysis with EPIC are presented in Table B-1-1. (Coincidentally, the USLE R factor is equal to 425 for all sites.)

The model was loaded with data from various sources, particularly the soil studies by A. Vásquez (pers. com., 1990). With a simulation of 20 years without erosion, soil productivity was estimated in each case under existing conditions. The estimated yields from the model are shown in Table B-1-2 under original soil conditions as well as from observations in the field for similar sites in Costa Rica. The estimated yields from the model varied considerably from the field results. The model could be adjusted to obtain more precise results, but doing so would require technical manipulation beyond the scope of this project.

Next, the model was used to estimate the impact of erosion over time. The model can simulate an episode of erosion, then stop to estimate average production during a subsequent 20-year period without erosion. Figure

Table B-1-1. Site Characteristics, Productivity Loss Depreciation

Site	Crop	Precipitation/yr (mm/yr)	Soil Type[a]	Slope	Soil Depth (m)
La Suiza de Turrialba	Pasture	2,605	D-2	4%	1.2
La Suiza de Turrialba	Corn	2,605	D-2	4%	1.2
Tierra Blanca de Cartago	Potato	2,313	F-2-4	15%	2.0
Fabian Baudrit-Alajuela	Corn	1,951	C-1	3%	1.51
El Alto, Tres Rios de Cartago	Pasture	2,770	F-2-4	4%	1.65

a. See Annex B-2

Source: Personal files of A. Vásquez.

Table B-1-2. Production Before Erosion: EPIC Model Estimates vs. Field Studies

Site	Crop	Yield, Estimated with EPIC Model[a]	Yield, Measured in Field
La Suiza de Turrialba	Pasture	0.40	2.8[b]
La Suiza de Turrialba	Corn	6.75	2.3[c]
Tierra Blanca de Cartago	Potato	7.83	41.4[d]
Fabio Baudrit-Alajuela	Corn	8.34	2.3[c]
El Alto, Tres Rios de Cartago	Pasture	0.54	2.8[b]

a. Average during 20-year period without erosion in original soil, in t/ha/yr.
b. Thousands of liters of milk/ha, Osvaldo C. Rockenbach, ''Análisis dinámico de dos sistemas de finca predominantes en el Cantón de Turrialba, Costa Rica'' Master's Thesis, Centro Agronómico Tropical de Investigación y Enseñanza (CATIE), San José, Costa Rica, 1981, pp. 54, 59.
c. Centro Agronómico Tropical para la Investigación y Enseñanza, Departamento de Producción Vegetal, *Alternativa de manejo para el sistema maíz-maíz* (Pococí-Guácimo, Costa Rica), 1984.
d. Values from production cost estimate for 1989–91, Ministry of Agriculture (C. Ramírez, MAG, pers. com., 1991).

B-1-1 depicts the deterioration of productivity over a century. In the two pasture cases, the model does not estimate any loss. In one case, this result is consistent with the analysis of nutrient loss, considering that ranching in Tres Rios causes less erosion than the maximum tolerable value presented in Table B-1-4. The inconsistencies for La Suiza could be due to light grazing and the omission from the model of typical Costa Rican ranching problems, such as soil compaction.

EPIC's economic submodel allows users to calculate net rent from the soil in different periods. Since the operations simulated in the EPIC model are mechanized, while typical operations in Costa Rica are manual, interpreting the results is difficult. Future studies may improve this aspect of the model.

Erosion-induced productivity losses cause a simultaneous decline in revenues and costs that vary with the harvest. The annual rent per

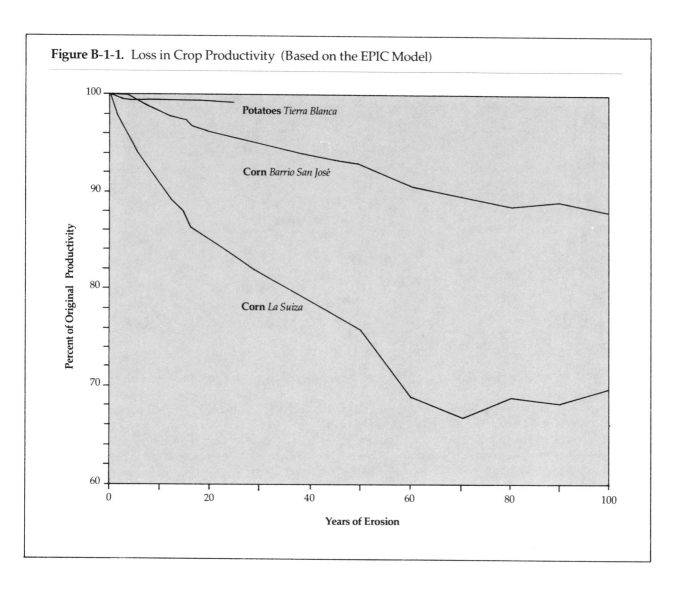

Figure B-1-1. Loss in Crop Productivity (Based on the EPIC Model)

hectare, therefore, declines. This annual loss is then capitalized to determine the value of the total resource depreciation.

To calculate the true cost of declining productivity, therefore, farm level budgets are necessary. Table B-1-3 presents a summary of budgets for the three crops studied. Since only limited information was available, the only

value considered to vary with production is the harvest labor.

Table B-1-4 presents the estimated percentage decline in annual yields for crop-sites, the annual value per hectare, and the asset losses due to erosion. Depreciation is very sensitive to the value of the land. Small percentage losses on valuable lands can be important

Table B-1-3. Farm Budgets Used to Calculate Value of Productivity Losses in Costa Rica (1984 colones/ha)

	Corn[b]	Pasture[c]	Potatoes[d]
Fixed labor costs[a]	6,140	1,460	39,376
Variable labor costs[a]	3,070	1,496	16,500
Factor inputs	4,805	3,378	311,413
Interest and land use	3,344	4,868	55,150
Total fixed costs[a]	14,289	9,706	405,939
Total variable costs[a]	3,070	1,496	16,500
Total fixed and variable costs[a]	17,359	11,201	422,438
Total production	2,359.8 kg/ha	2,821.3 lt/ha	41,400 kg/ha
Revenue[e]	22,711	11,968	671,342
Annual rent	5,352	767	248,904
Asset value/ha	89,200	12,777	4,148,399

Note: Assumes 6 percent discount rate.

a. Fixed and variable in this table refer only to the relationship of the costs to the volume harvested.
b. Values from Centro Agronómico Tropical de Investigación y Enseñanza, *Alternativa de manejo para el sistema maíz-maíz,* (Pococí-Guácimo, Costa Rica, 1984).
c. Values from Osvaldo C. Rockenbach, Análisis dinámico de dos sistemas de finca predominates en el Cantón de Turrialba, Costa Rica, ''Master's Thesis, Centro Agronómico Tropical de Investigación y Enseñanza (CATIE), San José, Costa Rica, 1981. Average of two dairy farms weighted in proportion to their total areas.
d. Values from production cost estimates of the Ministry of Agriculture for 1989–91 (C. Ramírez, MAG, pers. com., 1990).
e. Unit values for 1984 calculated as the average value of each crop as presented in Banco Central de Costa Rica, *Cifras sobre producción agropecuaria, 1978–1987,* San José, Costa Rica, 1989.

Table B-1-4. Value of the Loss in Soil Productivity (in 1984 colones)

Crop—Site	Decline in prod. due to erosion[a]	Annual Economic Rents/ha[b]	Loss in Annual Rents Due to Erosion	Decline in Asset Value[c]
Pasture—Suiza	0.00%	766.6	0.0	0.0
Corn—Suiza	1.63%	5,352.0	320.2	5,335.8
Potatoes—Tierra Blanca	0.13%	248,903.9	851.3	14,188.3
Corn—Barrio San José	0.03%	6,321.7	5.9	98.2
Pasture—Tres Rios	0.00%	1,043.9	0.0	0.0

a. Estimate of the impact of one year of erosion on total annual yields made using the EPIC model. See Figure B-1-1.
b. From Table B-1-3.
c. Assumes a 6% discount rate.

economically, compared with higher percentage losses for less valuable crops.

Implications for Future Studies

When estimates of land depreciation based on productivity loss are compared with estimates for the same lands using the nutrient loss method, in two of the five cases studied the nutrient loss method gave more conservative results than the EPIC model. Two other cases showed the opposite result, and, in one case, both models estimated no loss during the period. (See Table B-1-5.)

The last column of Table B-1-5 shows the percentage loss of productivity implied by the nutrient loss method. For example, in the case of corn in La Suiza, the value of lost nutrients is ¢1.9 thousand, equivalent to a 0.59 percent depreciation in annual productivity. In no case does the value of nutrients lost exceed that of a 1 percent loss in productivity.

Table B-1-5. Depreciation: EPIC Model vs. Nutrient Loss Method (in 1984 colones)

Crop	Site	EPIC[a]	Nutrient Loss[b]	Equivalent Productivity Loss[c]
Pasture	La Suiza	0.0	10.9	0.01%
Corn	La Suiza	5,335.8	1,917.9	0.59%
Potatoes	Tierra Blanca	14,188.3	861.3	0.01%
Corn	Barrio San José	98.2	971.3	0.30%
Pasture	Tres Rios	0.0	0.0	0.00%

a. Data from Table B-1-4.
b. Calculated for specified sites using the methodology described in the Soils Accounts Section.
c. The percentage decline in total annual yields which would imply asset depreciation equal to that estimated using the nutrient loss method.

Annex B-2
Land Unit Types

The land units described here are presented as groups of diverse cartographic units from the 1989 soil map at 1:200,000 scale, produced by Vásquez for the Ministerio de Agricultura y Ganadería (MAG)—Food and Agriculture Organization of the United Nations (FAO) Soil Conservation Project (1989). Soils were grouped on the basis of chemical, physical, and morphological characteristics, as well as management practices and land use.

A. Tropical Dry Alluvial Soil

These are flat lands, with deep fertile soils, medium to heavy in texture, and suitable for most of the region's crops. Precipitation is normally less than 2,000 mm annually, but with a marked three- to six-month dry season. The mean annual temperature exceeds 18°C.

These soils are subdivided according to drainage characteristics:

A-1 *Well Drained to Moderately Well Drained Soils.* These lands are flat, with deep, moderately fertile to fertile soils, medium to moderately heavy in texture, and suitable for most of the region's crops. The soils include Ustropepts, Haplustolls and level Haplustalfs on level relief.

A-2 *Poorly Drained Soils.* These soils occur in flat to flat-concave relief, are moderately deep to deep, fertile, moderately heavy to heavy in texture, poorly permeable, and badly drained. They include soils such as Tropaquepts and Tropaquents on level relief.

A-3 *Heavy Textured Soils.* This unit includes the nation's Vertisols, which are deep, moderately drained, clayey, slowly permeable, and have little structure. They include principally the Pellusterts and Pelluderts.

B. Tropical Moist Alluvial Soils

These soils occur on relatively flat terrain, are moderately fertile to fertile, moderately fine to heavy in texture, variable in depth depending mainly on drainage. These areas have a mean monthly temperature of 22°C, and average annual precipitation, evenly distributed throughout the year, exceeds 2,000 mm.

According to their drainage, they are subdivided into:

B-1 *Well or Moderately Drained Soils.* These soils are deep, well structured, fertile to moderately fertile, though with low to moderate organic matter content. They include such soils as Dystropepts, Eutropepts, Humitropepts, and Tropofluvents on level relief.

B-2 *Poorly Drained Soils.* These soils are shallow to moderately deep, fertile, fine to moderately fine in texture, with low to moderate organic matter content. Usually, problems with effective depth are associated with gleization and elevated freatic levels; many of these soils have water at or above the surface most of the year. This category includes such soils as Troposaprists, Tropaquepts, and Tropaquents.

C. Piedmont Lands and Gently Rolling Quaternary Terraces

These lands consist of relatively gently rolling soils, on 2 percent to 15 percent slopes. Distributed over the humid and dry tropics, they include:

C-1 *Piedmont and Gently Rolling Quaternary Terraces, Dry Tropics.* These soils are deep, well drained, well structured, brownish to reddish brown, with moderate to low organic matter content, and moderate to moderately heavy in texture, occasionally with a low to medium content of rocks on the surface and throughout the profile. The climatological characteristics are the same as for tropical dry soils. They include Ustropepts of gently rolling relief, Haplustolis, Haplustalfs, Palehumults, and Haplustults soils.

C-2 *Piedmont and Gently Rolling Quaternary Terraces, Humid Tropics.* These soils are moderately deep to deep, brownish or brown, heavy textured, well structured with good drainage, but somewhat less fertile than tropical dry soils because they leach more nutrients. They may present low to medium content of course fragments.

This category includes the following soils: gently rolling Dystropepts, Europepts, Humitropepts, Tropohumults, Palenumults, and Tropoudults.

D. Sloped and Moderately Rolling Quaternary Terraces

This category includes residual soils and quaternary terraces of moderately rolling relief, with 15 percent to 30 percent slopes. This land is divided into dry and humid tropics.

D-1 *Dry Tropical.* These soils are deep, well structured, moderately heavy to heavy in texture, well drained, brownish or brownish red, and fertile to moderately fertile but with slight to moderate erosion problems. This category includes the following soils: moderately rolling Ustropepts, Haplustalfs, Palehumults, and Haplustults.

D-2 *Humid Tropical.* These soils are deep, well drained, well structured, brownish yellow or reddish, highly leached, low to moderately fertile, and slightly to moderately eroded. This category includes moderately rolling Dystropepts, Humitropepts, Tropohumults and Tropoudults.

E. Strongly Rolling Residual Soils

This category includes soils that developed in place on strongly rolling terrain with 30 percent to 60 percent slopes. As in the previous categories, soils developed under tropical dry conditions are differentiated from those developed in humid tropical conditions.

E-1 *Severely Rolling Residual Soils in Dry Tropics.* These are shallow, well structured, coarse, reddish soils, often moderately to severely eroded. They are moderately fertile, and their external drainage is excessive, especially when under agricultural use. Severely rolling Ustropepts, Haplustalfs, and Haplustults soils belong to this category.

E-2 *Severely Rolling Residual Soils in Humid Tropics.* These resemble the dry tropical soils, but are reddish yellow, more leached, less fertile, and usually less eroded but susceptible to erosion if improperly used. Dystropepts on strongly rolling relief, Humitropepts, Tropohumults, and Tropodults belong to this group.

F. Soils Derived from Volcanic Ash (Pyroclastus or Pyroclastic Materials)

Soils derived from tropical ash or pyroclastic materials are distributed through the Guanacaste and Central corridors, the Central Valley, the Coto Brus zone, and around the Atlantic and Northern plains between the Guácimo and Sarapiquí rivers. They can be subdivided by physical characteristics and relief.

F-1 *Containing Irreversibly Dry Clays.* These soils developed on and in the foothills of the volcanic corridors in a temperate and constantly rainy climate. They are in moderate to strongly rolling relief, with slopes of 15 percent to 60 percent. They are deep, dark, rich in organic materials, moderately fertile and well drained. Their structure is good but fragile; only short dry spells can irreversibly dry out clay deposits into sand and silt-sized aggregate, leading to compaction, degradation, and erosion.

This category includes soils in two principal relief classes with limitations and aptitudes of use. The soils are defined as Hydrandepts of moderately and strongly rolling relief.

F-2 *Containing No Irreversible Clay Deposits.* These soils derived from volcanic ash that contains no or insignificant amounts of irreversibly drying clays. They are distributed in areas with a marked dry season (Central Valley) or rainy tropical conditions (southern and western foothills of the Guanacaste and Central Corridors, Coto Brus zone, in the Atlantic and Northern plains between the Guácimo and Sarapiquí rivers). The soils are deep, medium in texture, porous, well drained, well structured, dark brown to brown, moderately fertile but quite productive.

According to relief and climate conditions, these soils are further subdivided.

F-2-1 *Flat tropical humid soils.* These are distributed in the Atlantic and Northern plains between Guácimo and Puerto Viejo of Sarapiquí. They present slopes of less than 2 percent. They include principally the Dystrandepts (Hapludands) on the level relief of the Atlantic and north of the country.

F-2-2 *Flat tropical dry soils.* These soils are distributed in the Central Valley and small areas of the Pacific north on less than 2 percent slopes. They include Dystrandepts on level relief in the Central Valley and Pacific North.

F-2-3 *Gently to moderately rolling tropical humid soils.* These soils are distributed over the northern and eastern edges of the Central and Guanacaste corridors, respectively, as well as in the Coto Brus zone, on 2-percent to 30-percent slopes. In these climatic conditions, they are represented by Dystrandepts classes of gently and moderately rolling relief.

F-2-4 *Gently and moderately rolling tropical dry soil.* These soils occur in the southern and eastern foothills of the Central and Guanacaste corridors, respectively, as well as the Central Valley, on 2-percent to 30 percent slopes. They are represented by Dystrandepts of gently and moderately rolling relief.

F-2-5 *Strongly rolling tropical humid soils.* These soils are associated with gently and moderately rolling lands in the same regions but on 30 percent to 60 percent slopes. They are represented here by Dystrandepts on strongly rolling terrain.

F-2-6 *Strongly rolling tropical dry soils.* These soils are also associated with tropical dry soils on gently and moderately rolling land in the same regions but on 30 percent to 60 percent slopes. They are represented by Dystrandepts on strongly rolling relief.

G. Protected Lands

These soils are found on steep slopes (over 60 percent) or on severely eroded land with exposed base rock in many areas. This land is useless for agriculture or forestry and should be earmarked for protection or recreation. These soils are subdivided.

G-1 *Deep Residual Soils.* These include Dystrapepts, Halustalfs, Tropohumults, and Haplustults soils on steep and broken terrain.

G-2 *Medium Texture Volcanic Soils.* This category consists of strandepts and Hydrandepts soils on steep and broken land.

G-3 *Extremely Light Textured Volcanic Soils.* The main soil type in this category is Vitrandept on steep slopes.

G-4 *Superficial Soils.* This class is composed of Ustrorthents and Troporthents soils on steep slopes.

Annex B-3
Nitrogen, Potassium, and Phosphorous Levels Used in Estimating Nutrient Loss Through Erosion
Elemer Bornemisza

The nutrient loss method was based on maps of available nutrients in Costa Rican soils by Bertsch (1987). The result of thousands of soil analyses by the Ministry of Agriculture, this information was the source for the P and K evaluations. N was evaluated using the following calculations and data on organic material content from the Costa Rican soil map project and other information from the files of Alexis Vásquez.

Using the data on organic matter content for various representative soils, the value of the organic matter (OM) was converted into organic carbon (OC). The factor of 0.58, from soil science texts, was used in the calculation (Donahue and associates, 1977). The relation between OC and total nitrogen (OC/N_{tot}) varied between 10 and 20. Using an average of 15, the following was calculated:

$$N_{tot} = (MO \cdot 0.58)/15 = MO \cdot 0.039.$$

According to the authors cited, between 3 percent and 5 percent of total N is mineralized each year. Available nitrogen (N_{av}) is 0.195 percent of the organic material. A loss of 100 tons of soil containing 5 percent organic material implies an estimated loss of 9.75 kg of N_{av}. Volcanic soils are a special case; mineralization of organic material is about a third slower than the common mineralization.

The results of Bertsch (1987) were used to calculate available P loss by multiplying the $\mu g/ml$ of P extracted with Olsen's solution converted to kg/ton of soil. This measure of available P, which is much smaller than total P, is the acceptable guide for fertilization.

Similarly, K loss is calculated from interchangeable K, usually considered the main source of available K (Bertsch, 1987).

K values in meq/ml are converted to g/t by:

meq/100 ml = 10 meq/kg = 390 mg/kg = 3.9 g/t.

Notes

1. Of course, both soil (agricultural land) and standing timber (harvesting rights) are exchanged in the marketplace, but the conceptual problem runs much deeper.

2. Values for both income and export earnings are for 1989. Employment values are from 1987.

3. Suitability in this context implies neither over- nor underuse of the land, as defined by the Land Use Capacity System of the Tropical Science Center (TSC, 1985).

4. The balance of payments deficit is here defined as the "basic" balance on current account, direct investment, and other long-term capital. The depreciation of natural resource assets is quantified as an annual percentage of GDP.

5. In 1984 values.

6. This estimate is based on a range of incremental capital-output ratios of 2.5 to 3.0.

7. For further information about the history of Costa Rica's forests, *see* Tosi (1974).

8. Pulp and paper are excluded because they are not yet a true forest industry in Costa Rica.

9. Manuel Gomez, CATIE (Centro Agronómico Tropical para la Investigación y Enseñanza) pers. com., (Oct 1990).

10. Luis F. Sage, CANEFOR (Cámara Nacional de Empresarios Forestales) pers. com. (Oct 1990).

11. The forest's other values include its serving as wildlife habitat and tourist attraction. A recent study by Tobias and Mendelsohn (1991) measured the ecotourism value of the Monteverde Cloud Forest Biological Reserve in Costa Rica, based on visitors' willingness to incur travel costs to see the site. The ecotourism value was estimated at about $1,250 per hectare for the 10,000 hectare reserve. Although substantial, this value cannot be directly applied to all forest hectarage since it reflects the special characteristics of the Reserve.

12. Maps for land use were also available for 1977–78 and 1987, but were not used due to problems of compatibility between the maps. For example, the SEPSA map for 1977–78 is general and only large sectors of land uses such as pastures are recognizable.

    The different maps were digitized at CATIE, using the geographic information system ERDAS, and were converted to the format ARC/INFO and "cleaned" at the TSC Center for Geographic Information. The conversion was made with a program written for this project (Badilla, 1990), which transformed ERDAS exit files, in ASCII, into ARC/INFO entrance files. The land use and land unit maps were then overlaid digitally, yielding detailed information on the predominant physical conditions in each land use.

13. Landefeld and Hines (1982), demonstrate that if scarcity rents of unexploited resources increase at a rate equal to the discount rate, the unit rent is equal to the value of the depreciation of the resource due to the loss of one unit. Futhermore, if the resource is being mined, it is known that in equilibrium these rates should, in fact, be equal. In the case of Costa Rica, historically, the resource has been mined with very little regeneration following harvests. Results of the stumpage value analysis, show that the unit rents from timber in Costa Rica from 1970–89 increased at an average annual rate of 7.2 percent. Thus, stumpage value is a very close approximation of the true unit value of depreciation in Costa Rica.

14. More commonly used is the border price, which represents the economic opportunity cost. National price data were however, more detailed and permitted disaggregation of the wood classes to include many secondary species not reflected in such international data as the FAO Forest Products Annual.

15. Calculations from the stumpage value model were corroborated with results from other studies from various years, 1971 (Clavijo, 1972, and Rodríguez, 1972), 1976 (Villasuso, 1978) and 1980 (Veiman, 1982).

16. The Costa Rican sawmills are concentrated primarily in the Central Valley. This has led to diminished stumpage values and has limited the number of marketable species. According to Flores (1985, p. 96), "...the location of the forestry industry in the Central Valley has represented a significant national social cost."

17. The percent of marketable volume in years after 1989 was calculated using the function:
(% marketable in year t) = (% in year $t-1$)$^{0.98}$.

18. A notable exception is that of "laurel" (*Cordia alliadora*) which farmers often leave standing in the fields to sell later for sawmilling.

19. The resulting 1989 total is in line with other estimates based on cattle surveys (Alexis Vásquez, pers. com., 1990).

20. Magrath and Arens (1989) discuss a variety of different impacts that erosion can have upon soil productivity as technology evolves.

21. It is assumed that VSD is positive, that is, that the soil is depreciating. Theoretically, if marginal costs were greater than marginal revenues, declining yields would actually increase the value of the land. Such conditions, however, are not likely in practice.

22. This knowledge must be acquired from research or productivity models like the Rio Urachiche river basin study in Venezuela. That study used an agronomic model, relating soil erosion to productivity loss due to nitrogen depletion and loss of moisture retention (CIDIAT, CONARE, 1981, p. 12).

23. This is a necessary but insufficient criterion. The loss of productive capacity is due not only to nutrient content but also to density, capacity to support plant life, and other factors. Overall, nutrient value is a minimal estimate of soil depreciation.

24. The land use estimates for the period 1963–1989 are consistent with those utilized in the Forestry Accounts. A more indepth discussion of the land use estimates is presented in the physical accounts section of the forestry accounts above.

25. Crops that cannot be used sustainably in the soil type are not taken into account.

26. Take, for example, a particular soil type that could be sustainably utilized under

annual crops (C value 0.34) with terracing (P factor 0.14,) or perennial crops (C factor 0.86), using less intensive management practices (say, factor 0.6). The sustainable C • P value for annual crops for this soil is 0.0476, while the same value for perennial crops is greater, 0.0516. Perennial crops therefore represent a more erosive sustainable use of this soil, and the C • P factor of 0.0516 was used to calculate the soil's sustainable erosion level.

27. In other words, for 1 kg of nitrogen lost, 50 g of mineralized nitrogen are lost each year thereafter until lost organic material is replaced through soil conservation practices and natural soil regeneration.

28. Nitrogen was expressed in terms of urea, phosphorous in terms of triple superphosphate, and potassium in terms of potassium muriate. Pure nutrient was converted to fertilizer volume by dividing by the nutrient of the fertilizer, and by the efficiency of fertilizer use in Costa Rica. The efficiency of fertilizer refers to the percentage of fertilizer that does not wash away or leach into the soil due to climatic conditions.

29. The remaining years were estimated using the wholesale price index for fertilizers. FERTICA's prices are controlled by law and do not necessarily cover all production costs.

30. Hartshorn and associates (1982, p. 58) estimate "the combined hydric and animal caused erosion on pasture lands in *wet forest* life zone climatic conditions might be between 400 and 800 metric tons/ha/year."

31. All economic values in this section are 1985 colones (¢) at the exchange rate of ¢50.45 = US$1.00. Unit value for kwh = ¢0.191, using the average costs of national hydroelectric plants (Rodrïguez, p. 110). Using thermal energy costs, the unit value is ¢2.74/kwh.

32. All tonnage in this section is in metric tons (mt).

33. An important exception is the sardine fleet, which grew rapidly in the early 1970s but collapsed in the latter half of the decade, and by 1980 had almost entirely shut down.

34. See, for example, *Estrategia de conservación para el desarrollo sostenible de Costa Rica*, MIRENEM, (Ministerio de Recursos Naturales, Energía y Minas) 1990[b].

35. A discussion of the relationship between mangrove area and shrimp production is presented in Section D.

36. See Pauly (1980, p. 34) for a discussion of various models. This simple model implicitly assumes that the biological and environmental conditions of the fishery do not change during the period.

37. Rent *equals* total revenue *less* total cost, including return on capital. Labor costs in natural resource account analysis should be valued at the opportunity cost level because wages above the shadow price are equivalent to rents attributable to the resource.

38. Andres Gomez-Lobo (1990) used a net price valuation of the changes in the biomass of two fish species in Chile to estimate the depreciation of the fishery resource. While the limitations of using biomass efforts instead of yield estimates should be considered, there is no single valid method for determining fishery depreciation.

39. In 1987, as mentioned in *Diagnóstico del sector pesquero de Costa Rica*, NORAD/FAO/OLDEPESCA (1990, p. 76).

40. Average for 1986 and 1987 based on unpublished data, Dirección General de Recursos Pesqueros y Acuacultura.

41. Because boats over 10-m long are not allowed to fish in the inner Gulf, these 56

censused boats were excluded from the estimate of effort level. The raw data was further adjusted to eliminate vessels with identical names and specifications.

42. *Fishing efficiency* here is total catch/kw-day.

43. For a discussion of these relationships see, for example, Pauly (1980).

44. R^2 = 0.854 Standard error = 0.0000238.

45. Pablo Acevedo Ruiz, Dirección de Pesca, Puntarenas; Pedro Mendoza, Cámara de Pescadores Artesenales; and Gilbert Brenes Leon, Coopeimpesca, (a fishing supply cooperative), pers. com., 1990.

46. A 6 percent real interest rate was used throughout this study, as explained in the forestry accounts.

47. Calculated from the 1984 Population Census using the 10.9 percent unemployment rate in cantons along the Gulf of Nicoya instead of the 7.1 percent national rate.

48. As in the forestry accounts of Repetto and associates (1989).

49. The basal area fluctuates between 4 m² and 30 m²/ha, and the peaks rarely exceed 20 m (Jiménez and Soto, 1985, Jiménez, 1990).

50. The volume was calculated, for strata where *Avicennia* predominated, by:
$$\log_{10} vol = -4.4267 + 1.15748\, lnx,$$
and for strata where *Rhizophora* predominated, by:
$$ln\, vol = -0.89139 + 2.49076\, lnx,$$
where x is diameter at breast height of the tree. (COHDEFOR Corporación Hondureña de Desarrollo Forestal, 1987.) These volume estimates pertain to technically unmanaged mangrove forests.

51. Salazar (1986, p. 86) reports 7,460 Kcal/kg, 1.55 percent residues, in mangrove charcoal and humidity level of only 9.5 percent.

52. For example, the *Anadara tuberculosa* gathered by the Indians were 20 percent larger than today's average mollusk (R.A. Cruz, pers. com., 1990).

53. PNSA (1989, p. 57) reports construction costs of $3,049/ha for operations of 5 ha, and daily costs of $9.75.

References

BCCR, Banco Central de Costa Rica. 1990. Indices de precios al por mayor, sub-grupo materiales de construcción, sub-grupo materiales de madera. Departamento de Indices, Sección de Cuentas Sociales, San José, Costa Rica. Unpublished data.

_____ 1989a. *Cifras sobre producción agropecuaria 1978–1987*. Departamento de Contabilidad Social, San José.

_____ 1989b. *Estadísticas del sector industrial manufacturero 1978–1987*. Departamento de Contabilidad Social, San José.

_____ 1989c. *Principales estadísticas sobre las transacciones de Costa Rica en el extranjero, 1985*. San José, Costa Rica.

_____ 1986. *Estadísticas 1950–1985*, División Económica, San José, Costa Rica.

Badilla, H. 1990. Program to Convert GIS Files in ASCII from ERDAS Files to ARC/INFO (PASCAL). Tropical Science Center, San José, Costa Rica. Not distributed.

Bennett, H.H. 1939. *Soil Conservation*, New York: McGraw Hill.

Bertsch, F. 1987. *Manual para interpretar la fertilidad de los suelos de Costa Rica*, 2d.ed. San José: Escuela de Fitotecnica, Universidad de Costa Rica. 80 pp.

Biot, Y.J. 1988. "Modelling Productivity Losses Caused by Erosion." *Proceedings of the Fifth International Soil Conservation Conference*, Department of Land Development, Ministry of Agriculture and Cooperatives, Bangkok, Thailand, 18–19 Jan. 1988, pp. 177–96.

Blaser, J. 1987. "Standortliche und Waldbauliche Analyse eines Eichenwolkenwaldes (Querqus sp.) der Montanstufe in Costa Rica. Göttinger Beiträge zur Land-und Forstwirtschaft in den Tropen und Subtropen." Dissertation, Forstliche Fakultät, Universität Göttinger, Germany.

Bockor, I. 1977. "Analyze von Baumartenzussammensetzung und Bestandesstrukturen eines andinen Wolkenwaldes in West Venezuela als Grundlage zur Waldtypengliederung." Doctoral Dissertation, Forstliche Fakultät, Universität Göttinger, Germany.

Brown, S. 1984. "Biomass of Tropical Forests: A New Estimate Based on Forest Volumes." *Science* 223 (Mar.): 1290–93.

Brown, S., and A. Lugo. 1990. Tropical Secondary Forests. *Journal of Tropical Ecology* 6:1–32.

CAAP, Consejo Agrícola y Agroindustrial Privado. 1987. *A Study of the Potential for Commercial Pond Aquaculture in Costa Rica*. Report to the United States Agency for

International Development (USAID), Aquatic Systems, Inc. San Diego, Calif.

CATIE, Centro Agronómico Tropical de Investigación y Enseñanza. 1984. *Alternativa de manejo para el sistema maíz-maíz*, Pococí-Guácimo, Costa Rica.

Chacón H., R., and O. Gamboa J. 1989. *Boletín Estadístico*, no. 3. Dirección General Forestal, Departamento de Planificación, San José, Costa Rica.

Chong, P.W. 1988. *Forest Management Plan for Playa Garza Pilot Area: Terraba-Sierpe Mangrove Reserve*. Report prepared for the Government of the Republic of Costa Rica by the Food and Agriculture Organization of the United Nations (FAO), San José, Costa Rica. FAO-DGF (Dirección General Forestal) Technical Report 3, July.

Chudnoff, Martin. 1974. "Influence of Climatic Life Zones on Density of Tropical Timbers." Forest Products Laboratory, Forest Service, U.S. Department of Agriculture. Madison, Wisconsin.

CIDIAT, Centro Internacional de Desarrollo Integral de Tierras y Aguas/CONARE, Consejo Nacional de Rectores. 1981. "Estudio de impacto ambiental del proyecto de manejo conservacionista de las microcuencas de Cocorotico y el Tejar." USB/CONARE-FCA. Merida, Venezuela.

Clavijo B., Armando. 1972. "Análisis de costos de arrastre en bosque homogeneo natural de Costa Rica." Master of Science Thesis, Instituto Interamericano de Ciencias Agrícolas de la OEA, CATIE, Departamento de Ciencias Forestales Tropicales, Turrialba, Costa Rica.

COHDEFOR, Corporación Hondureña de Desarrollo Forestal. 1987. "Inventario Forestal Manglar del Sur, Golfo de Fonseca." Report to the United States Agency for International Development/World Wildlife Fund/Asociación Hondureña de Ecología, Tegucigalpa, Honduras.

CORENA, Conservación de Recursos Naturales/MAG, Ministerio de Agricultura y Ganadería. 1984. "Plan de manejo de la Cuenca del Rio Parrita." MAG, San José, Costa Rica.

Cruz W.; H.A. Francisco; Q. Tapwan-Conway. 1988. "The On-Site and Downstream Costs of Soil Erosion in the Magath and Pantabangan Watersheds." *Journal of Philippine Development* 15(1).

D'Croz, L., and B. Kwiecinski. 1980. "Contribución de los manglares a las pesquerias de la bahía de Panamá." *Revista de Biología Tropical* 28(1): 13–29.

Dickinson, J.; J. Bustillo, J.A. Jiménez, C. Onuf, D. Rouse, J. Varela, E. Villega. 1985. "Environmental Assessment of the Small Scale Shrimp Farming Component of the USAID/Honduras Rural Technologies Project." Report to USAID-Honduras, supervised by Tropical Research and Development, Inc., Gainesville, FL.

Dirección de Geología, Minas y Petróleo. 1982. "Mapa Geológico de Costa Rica, escala 1:200,000." San José, Costa Rica.

Dirección General de Estadística y Censos. 1987a. *Censo Agropecuario 1984*. Ministerio de Industria y Comercio, San José, Costa Rica.

_____ 1987b. *Censo de Población 1984*. Ministerio de Industria y Comercio, San José, Costa Rica.

_____ 1974. *Censo Agropecuario 1973*. Ministerio de Industria y Comercio, San José, Costa Rica.

_____ 1966. *Censo Agropecuario 1963*. Ministerio de Industria y Comercio, San José, Costa Rica.

DGF, Dirección General Forestal. 1988. *Censo de la industria forestal 1986–87*. Departamento de Desarrollo Industrial, San José, Costa Rica, (1975, 1980, 1986, 1987).

_____ 1984. *Proyecto producción forestal Sarapiquí*, vols. 1–5. Departamento de Desarrollo Industrial, San José, Costa Rica.

_____ 1982. *Censo de la Industria de Aserrio 1980*, Departamento de Economía y Industria Forestal, San José, Costa Rica.

Donahue, R.L.; R.W. Miller, and J.C. Shickluna. 1977. *Soils: An Introduction to Soils and Plant Growth*, 4th ed. New York: Prentice-Hall.

Finegan, B., and C. Sabogal. 1988a. El desarrollo de sistemas de producción sostenible en bosques tropicales húmedos de bajura: un estudio de caso en Costa Rica. *El Chasqui* 6(17):3–24, Centro Agronómico Tropical de Investigación y Enseñanza, Turrialba, Costa Rica.

_____ 1988b. El desarrollo de sistemas de producción sostenible en bosques tropicales húmedos de bajura: un estudio de caso en Costa Rica. *El Chasqui* 6(18):16–24, Centro Agronómico Tropical de Investigación y Enseñanza, Turrialba, Costa Rica.

Flores Rodas, José. 1985. *Diagnostico del Sector Industrial Forestal*. San José, Costa Rica: Editoral Universidad Estato a Distancia.

Fox, W.W. 1970. ''An Exponential Surplus-Yield Model for Optimizing Exploited Fish Populations. *Transactions of the American Fisheries Society* 99(1): 80–88.

Gómez-Lobo, Andrés. 1990. ''Desarrollo sostenible del sector pesquero chileno en los años 80.'' Unpublished paper, Corporación de Investigaciones Económicas para Latinoamerica, Santiago, Chile.

González-Moza, Rodrigo. 1976 ''Censo de aserraderos realizado durante enero y febrero 1975.'' *Technical Report* No. 5, Ministerio de Agricultura y Ganadería, Dirección General Forestal, Departamento Investigación Forestal, San José, Costa Rica.

Gregerson, H.; K.N. Brooks; J.A. Dixon, and L.S. Hamilton. 1988. *Conservation Guide*, ''Pautas para la evaluación económica de proyectos de ordenación de cuencas.'' Rome, Italy: FAO (Food and Agriculture Organization).

Gregory, G. 1976. *Forest Resource Economics*. New York, Ronald Press.

Hamilton, L.S., and P.N. King. 1983. *Tropical Forested Watershed–Hydrologic and Soil Response to Major Uses or Conversions*. Boulder, Col.: Westview Press.

Hamilton, L.S., and S.C. Snedaker. 1984. *Handbook for Mangrove Area Management*. Honolulu, Hawaii: Environment and Policy Institute, East-West Center/International Union for the Conservation of Nature and Natural Resources/United Nations Educational, Scientific and Cultural Organization/United Nations Environment Programme.

Hartshorn, G.L.; A. Atmella, L. Diego Gómez, A. Mata, R. Morales, R. Ocampo, D. Pool, C. Quesada, C. Solera, R. Solórzano, G. Stiles, J. Tosi, A. Umaña, C. Villalobos, R. Wells. 1982. *Costa Rica Country Environmental Profile*. San José, Costa Rica: TSC/USAID.

Hendrison, J. 1990. ''Damage-Controlled Logging in Managed Tropical Rain Forest in Suriname.'' Doctoral dissertation, Wageningen Agricultural University, Wageningen, Netherlands.

Herrera, R. 1990. ''Evaluación financiera del manejo del bosque natural secundario en cinco sitios en Costa Rica.'' Master's thesis, CATIE, Turrialba, Costa Rica.

Heheisel, H. 1976. ''Struktur uns Waldtypengliederung in Primaren Wolkenwald 'San Eusebio' in der Nordkordillere der venezolanischen Anden.'' Dissertation, University of Göttingen, Göttingen, Germany.

Holdridge, L.R. 1967. *Life Zone Ecology*. San José, Costa Rica: TSC.

Holdridge, L.R.; W.C. Grenke, W.H. Hathaway, T. Liang, J.A. Tosi. 1971. *Forest Environments in Tropical Life Zones: A Pilot Study.* Oxford, New York, Toronto, Sydney, Braunschweig: Pergamon Press.

IGN (Instituto Geográfico Nacional) 1987 "Mapa Físico Político de Costa Rica." Scale 1:400,000, San José, Costa Rica.

_____ 1985. "Mapa de Uso de la Tierra." Scale 1:200,000, San José, Costa Rica.

_____ 1984. "Mapa de Uso de la Tierra." Scale 1:200,000, San José, Costa Rica.

_____ 1970. "Mapa de Uso de la Tierra." Scale 1:200,000, San José, Costa Rica.

IMF, International Monetary Fund. 1991. *International Financial Statistics* 20:14 (15 Jul.).

Jiménez, J.A. 1990. "The Structure and Function of Dry Weather Mangroves on the Pacific Coast of Central America, with Emphasis on *Avicennia bicolor* Forests." *Estuaries* 13(2):182–92.

_____ 1988a. "Floral and Fruiting Phenology of Trees in a Mangrove Forest on the Dry Pacific Coast of Costa Rica." *Brenesia* 29: 33–50.

_____ 1988b. "The Dynamics of *Rhizophora racemosa* Forests on the Pacific Coast of Costa Rica." *Brenesia* 30:1–12.

_____ 1984. "A Hypothesis to Explain the Reduced Distribution of the Mangrove *Pelliciera Rhizophorae.*" *Biotropica* 16(4): 304–08.

Jiménez, J.A., and R. Soto. 1985. "Patrones regionales en la estructura y composición florística de los manglares de la costa Pacífica de Costa Rica." *Revista Biología Tropical* 33(1):25–37.

Kapetsky, J.; L. McGregor, and H. Nanne. 1987. "A Geographical Information System and Satellite Remote Sensing to Plan for Aquaculture Development." FAO (Food and Agriculture Organization of the United Nations) Fishery Technical Paper.

Lal, Rattan. 1987. "Effects of Soil Erosion on Crop Productivity." *CRC Critical Reviews in Plant Sciences* 5:4: 303–68.

_____ 1985. "Soil Erosion and Its Relation to Productivity in Tropical Soils." In S.A. El-Swaify W.C. Moldenhauer, A. Lo, eds., *Soil Erosion and Conservation.* Ankeney, Iowa: Soil Conservation Society of America.

Landefeld, J.S. & J.M. Hines 1982. Valuing non-renewable natural resources: the mining industries. In: *Measuring Nonmarket Economic Activity: BEA Working Papers*, Bureau of Economic Analysis.

Larson, W.E., F.J. Pierce and R.H. Dowdy. 1985. "Loss in Long-Term Productivity from Soil Erosion in the United States." In S.A. El-Swaify, W.C. Moldenhauer, A. Lo, eds., *Soil Erosion and Conservation.* Ankeney, Iowa: Soil Conservation Society of America.

Leonard, H.I. 1986. "Recursos naturales y desarrollo económico en América Central: un perfil ambiental regional." Trans. by G. Budowski and T. Maldonado. San José, Costa Rica: CATIE.

Linden, O., and A. Jernelov. 1980. "The Mangrove Swamp: An Ecosystem in Danger." *Ambio* 9(2): 81–88.

Lindsey, R.K.; M.A. Kohler, and J.L.H. Paulos. 1977. *Hidrología para Ingenieros*, 2 ed.. Trans. by A. Deeb, J. Ordoñez, and F. Catrillon. Bogotá, Colombia: McGraw Hill.

Lombardi, N.F., and J. Bertouni. 1975. "Tolerância de perdas de terra para solos de Estado de São Paulo." Boletín Técnico del Instituto Agronómico. 28: 1–12.

López Cadenas, Filiberto; Antonio Perez-Soba Baro; Jorge Aguilo Bonnin; Mariano Magister

Hafner; Filiberto López Sarda; José Maria Rapade Blaco; Carlos Copano Gonzalez de Heredia; Margarita Roldan Soriano; Jesús Gomez Parrondo; Joaquin Navarro Julian; José Luis Garcia Rodriguez, and Antonio Garcia Castaño. 1987. "Mapas de estados erosivos: cuenca hidrográfica del Tajo," Instituto Nacional para la Conservación de la Naturaleza, Ministerio de Agricultura, Pesca y Alimentación, Madrid, Spain.

Luna Lugo, A. 1976. "Aprovechamiento de manglares: un caso particular en Venezuela." *Curso Intensivo Sobre Manejo y Aprovechamiento de Bosques Tropicales.* Turrialba, Costa Rica: Organization of American States/CATIE.

Madrigal Abarca, Eduardo. 1985. "Dinámica pesquera de tres especies de *sciaenidae* corvinas en el Golfo de Nicoya, Costa Rica." Master of Science thesis, Universidad de Costa Rica, Facultad de Biología, San José, Costa Rica.

MAG, Ministerio de Agricultura y Ganadería. 1989. "Censo Sobre Embarcaciones, Pescadores y Artes de Pesca." Oficina Regional de Pesca de Puntarenas. Unpublished raw data.

Mahamood, K. 1987. "Reservoir Sedimentation." World Bank Technical Paper #71, p. 386.

Magrath, William and Peter Arens. 1989. "The cost of soil erosion on Java: A natural resource accounting approach." Environment Dept. Working Paper Series #18, World Bank, Washington, D.C.

Malavassi, L.; R. Alfaro; W. Murillo, and G. Herrera. 1986. "Evaluación del recurso biológico del manglar de Tivives." Report to Fundación de Parques Nacionales, Programa de Patrimonio Natural. San José, Costa Rica.

Malleux, J. 1982. *Inventarios Forestales en Bosques Tropicales.* La Molina, Peru: Universidad Agraria.

Marmillod, D. 1982. "Methodik und Ergebnisse von Untersuchungen über Zussammensetzung und Aufbau eines Terrassenwaldes in peruanischen Amazonien." Dissertation, Forstliche Fakultät, Universität Göttinger, Germany.

Mbagwu, J.S.C.; R. Lal, and T.W. Scott. 1984. "Effects of Desurfacing of Alfisols and Ultisols in Southern Nigeria—Crop Performance. *Soil Science Society of America Journal* 48 (4): 834–838.

Meléndez, C. 1974. "Viajeros por Guanacaste." Ministerio de Cultura, Juventud y Deportes. San José, Costa Rica.

Mercer, D.E., and L.S. Hamilton. 1984. "Algunas ventajas económicas y naturales de los ecosistemas de manglares." *Naturaleza y sus Recursos* 20(2): 14–19.

MIRINEM, Ministerio de Recursos Naturales, Energía y Minas. 1990a. *Plan de Acción Forestal para Costa Rica.* San José, Costa Rica: MIRINEM.

_____ 1990b. *Estrategia de conservación para el desarrollo sostenible de Costa Rica,* San José, Costa Rica.

Morales, T. 1983. "Evaluación de la extracción de corteza de mangle. Guanacaste." *Informe de practica de especialidad,* Instituto Tecnológico, Cartago, Costa Rica.

Moreira A., L., and E. Palma A. 1987. *Boletín Estadístico,* no. 2, Dirección General Forestal, Departamento de Planificación, San José, Cosa Rica.

NORAD/FAO/OLDEPESCA, Norwegian Agency for Development/Food and Agriculture Agency/ Organización Latinoamericano para el desarrollo de la Pesca. 1990. *Diagnóstico del Sector Pesquero de Costa Rica.* San José, Costa Rica: NORAD/FAO/OLDEPESCA.

Onstad, C.A., and R.A. Young. 1988. "System Analysis for Erosion Evaluation and Prediction."

Proceedings of the Fifth International Soil Conservation Conference. Department of Land Development, Ministry of Agriculture and Cooperatives, Bangkok, Thailand, 18–19 Jan. 1988, pp. 23–35.

Pauly, Daniel. 1980. *A Selection of Simple Methods for the Assessment of Tropical Fish Stocks*, Rome, Italy: U.N. Food and Agriculture Organization.

Pauly, D., and J. Ingles. 1986. "The Relationship Between Shrimp Yields and Intertidal Vegetation Areas: A Reassesment." In A. Yañez-Arancibia and D. Pauly, eds., IOC/FAO Workshop on Recruitment in Tropical Coastal Demersal Communities. IOC Workshop Report 44-Supplement. Ciudad del Carmen Campeche, Mexico.

PCCP-UNA, Programa de Capacitación a Comunidades Pesqueras, Universidad Nacional. 1987. "Evaluación de la extracción de pianguas en Jicaral-Puntarenas," Heredia, Costa Rica. Processed.

Pierce, F.J.; W.E. Larson, R.H. Dowdy, and W.A.P. Graham. 1983. "Productivity of Soils: Assessing Long Term Changes Due to Erosion." *Journal of Soil and Water Conservation* 38 (Jan–Feb):39–44.

PNSA. 1989. *Programa Nacional Sectorial de Acuacultura*. San José, Costa Rica: Ministerio de Agricultura y Ganadería.

Rehm, S. 1978. "Land Development in the Humid Tropics." Proceedings of International Symposium on Agricultural Mechanization of the German Agricultural Cooperative [Agra-Mechanisierung der Deutsche Landwärtschaft Gemeimschaft], Frankfurt, Germany.

Repetto, R.; W. Magrath, M. Wells, C. Beer, and F. Rossini. 1989. *Wasting Assets: Natural Resources in the National Income Accounts*. World Resources Institute, Washington, DC.

Rijaberman, F.R., and M.G. Woloman. 1985. "Effect of Erosion on Soil Productivity: An International Comparison." *Journal of Soil and Water Conservation* (Jul–Aug). pp. 349–54.

Rockenbach, Osvaldo C. 1981. "Análisis dinámico de dos sistemas de finca predominantes en el Cantón de Turrialba, Costa Rica" Master's thesis, CATIE, San José, Costa Rica, pp. 54, 59.

Rodríguez, Jorge. 1972. "Un modelo de predicción del tiempo requerido para el volteo y troceo con motosierra en un bosque humedo tropical." Master of Science thesis, Centro Agronómico Tropical de Investigación y Enseñanza, Departamento de Ciencias Forestales Tropicales, Turrialba, Costa Rica.

Rodríguez, R. 1989. "Impactos del uso de la tierra en la alteración del régimen de caudales, la erosión y sedimentación de la cuenca superior del río Reventazón y los efectos económicos en el proyecto hidroeléctrico de Cachí." Costa Rica. Master's thesis, CATIE, Turrialba, Costa Rica.

Rosenzweig, Michael L. 1968. "Net Primary Productivity of Terrestrial Communities: Prediction from Climatological Data." *American Naturalist* 102(923)67–73.

Sabogal, C. 1987. Struktur und Entwicklungs Dynamik eines-amazonischen Naturwaldes bei Pucallpa, Perú. Dissertation, Forstliche Fakultät, Universität Göttinger, Germany.

Salazar, R. 1986. "Estudio sobre producción y mercadeo de carbón vegetal." San José, Costa Rica. Unpublished paper.

Sánchez, R.O. 1986. "Metodología descriptiva para determinar las posibles usos de las áreas de manglares, y su aplicación en Coronado-Sierpe, Costa Rica." Masters thesis, CATIE, Turrialba, Costa Rica.

Sandner, G. 1972. *La Colonización Agrícola de Costa Rica*. Instituto Geográfico de Costa Rica, Ministerio de Obras Públicas y Transportes, San José, Costa Rica.

SEPSA, Secretaria de Planificación Sectorial Agropecuaria, FAO. 1986. El Sector Agropecuario: Diagnóstico. Doc.-SEPSA-107. San José, Costa Rica.

_____ 1990. Secretaria de Planificación Sectorial Agropecuaria, FAO. El Sector Agropecuario: Diagnóstico. San José, Costa Rica.

Sharpley, A.N., and J.R. Williams, eds. 1990. EPIC—Erosion/Productivity Impact Calculator—User Manual: U.S. Department of Agriculture Technical Bulletin No. 1768.

Shultz, E.F. 1980. *Problems in Applied Hydrology*. Fort Collins: Colorado State University.

Siew, T.K., and C. Fatt. 1976. *Effects of Simulated Erosion on Performance of Maize (Zea mays) Grown on Durian Series*. Soil Conservation Reclamation Report No. 3, Ministry of Agriculture, Kuala Lumpur, Malaysia.

Silvestre, Geronimo, and Daniel Pauly. "Estimate of Yield and Economic Rent from Philippine Demersal Stocks (1946–1984) Using Vessel Horsepower as an Index of Fishing Effort." *University of Philippines in the Visayas Fishery Journal* 1:2 (Jul–Dec 1985), 2:12 (Jan–Dec 1986) and 3:1–2 (Jan–Dec 1987).

Stevenson, David, and Francisco Carranza. 1981. "Maximum Yield Estimates for the Pacific Thread Herring, *Opisthonema Spp.* Fishery in Costa Rica." *Fishery Bulletin*: 79.

Stocking, M. 1988. "Quantifying the On-Site Impact of Soil Erosion." Proceedings of the Fifth International Soil Conservation Conference, Department of Land Development, Ministry of Agriculture and Cooperatives, Bangkok, Thailand, 18–19 Jan, pp. 137–61.

Swedforest Consulting AB. 1977. *Talamanca Forest Project*. Report to Agri-Science Resource and Development Corporation, Managua, Nicaragua, and to the Junta de Administración Portuaria y de Desarrollo Económico de la Vertiente Atlántica, San José, Costa Rica.

Thiel, S. A. 1902. Monografía de la población de Costa Rica en el siglo XIX. *Revista de Costa Rica en el Siglo XIX*. San José, Costa Rica.

Tobias, Dave and Robert Mendelsohn, "Valuing Ecotourism in a Tropical Rain-Forest Reserve," in *Ambio*, vol. 20, no. 2, April 1991.

Toro, V. 1978. "Mangrove Forest and Its Usefulness to Shrimp Fisheries in Indonesia." Paper presented to the Eighth World Forestry Congress, Jakarta, Indonesia.

Tosi, J. A., Jr. 1980a. "Life Zones, Land Use, and Forest Vegetation in the Tropical and Subtropical Regions," manuscript, TSC, San José, Costa Rica. Published under same title, but without formulation cited, in S. Brown, A. E. Lugo, and B. Liegel, eds. 1980. *The Role of Tropical Forests in the World Carbon Cycle*. U.S. Dept. of Energy, CONF-800350, National Technical Information Service, Springfield, Va.

_____. 1980b. *Estudio ecológico integral de las zonas de afectación del Proyecto Arenal*. San José, Costa Rica: TSC.

_____. 1974. *Los Recursos Forestales de Costa Rica, Acta Final*. Primer Congreso Nacional sobre Conservación de Recursos Naturales Renovables. San José: Facultad de Agronomía, Universidad de Costa Rica.

TSC, Tropical Science Center. 1990. "Map of the Lifezones of Costa Rica According to the Holdridge System, 1:200,000 Scale." San José, Costa Rica. In press.

_____ 1987. "Estudio del plan de manejo forestal de la Hacienda Copano S.A." Report to the Hacienda Copano Company, San José, Costa Rica, Jun.

_____ 1985. *Manual para la determinación de la capacidad de uso de las tierras de Costa Rica.* San José, Costa Rica: TSC.

Turner, R. E. 1977. "Intertidal Vegetation and Commercial Yields of *Penaeid* Shrimps. *Transactions of the American Fisheries Society* 106 (5): 411–416. Sept.

United Nations. 1975. *A System of National Accounts.* New York: UN.

_____ 1977. *Provisional International Guidelines on the National and Sectoral Balance Sheet and Reconciliation Accounts of the System of National Accounts,* Statistical Papers, Series M, no. 60.

UNESCO/UNEP/FAO, United Nations Educational, Scientific and Cultural Organization/ United Nations Environment Programme/ Food and Agriculture Organization of the United Nations. 1980. *Ecosistemas de los bosques tropicales. Informe del estado de los conocimientos.* Serie Investigación sobre Recursos Naturales XIV, Madrid, Spain.

Vahrson, W.G. 1989. "Mapa preliminar de la erosividad pluvial anual en Costa Rica, escala 1:1,000,000." Proyecto Morfoclimatología aplicada, y dinamica exógena. Escuela Ciencias Geográficas, Universidad Nacional, Heredia, Costa Rica.

Vásquez, A. 1989. "Cartografía y clasificación de suelos de Costa Rica (escala 1:200,000)." Proyecto "Apoyo al Servicio Nacional de Conservación de Suelos y Aguas" (GCP-COS-009-ITA). FAO, San José, Costa Rica.

Veillon, Jean P., and Associates. 1983. El Crecimiento de Algunos Bosques Naturales de Venezuela en Relación con los Parametros del Medio Ambiente. Instituto de Silvicultura, Universidad de los Andes, Merida, Venezuela.

Veiman Quinn, Charles S. 1982. "Plan Piloto para manejo forestal de los terrenos de J.A.P.D.E.V.A." (Junta de Administración Portuaria y de Desarrollo Económico de la Vertiente Atlántica), Master of Science thesis, Centro Agronómico Tropical de Investigación y Enseñanza, Departamento de Recursos Naturales Renovables, Turrialba, Costa Rica.

Villasuso E., Juan Manuel. 1978. El sector forestal y madero en Costa Rica. Oficina de Planificación y Política Económica de la Presidencia de la República (OFIPLAN), San José, Costa Rica.

Williams, J.R.; P.T. Dyke, W.W. Fuchs, V.W. Benson, O.W. Rice, and E.D. Taylor. 1990. EPIC Erosion/Productivity Impact Calculator: 2, User Manual. A.N. Sharpley and J.R. Williams, eds. U.S. Department of Agriculture Technical Bulletin No. 1768.

Williams, J.R., and K.G. Renard. 1985. "Assessments of Soil Erosion and Crop Productivity with Process Models (EPIC)." In R.F. Follett and B.A. Steward, eds., *Soil Erosion and Crop Productivity.* Madison, Wisconsin: American Society of Agronomy, Inc./ Crop Science Society of America, Inc./Soil Science Society of America, Inc.

Wischmeier, W.H., and D.D. Smith. 1978. "Predicting Rainfall Erosion Losses." *USDA Handbook.* Washington: U.S. Department of Agriculture, p. 537.

WRI, World Resources Institute. 1988. *World Resources 1988–89,* New York: Basic Books.

Yost, R.S.; S.A. El-Swaify; E.W. Dongler, and A. Lo. 1985. "The Influence of Simulated Soil Erosion and Restorative Fertilization of Maize Production in an Otisol." pp. 248–61 In *Soil Erosion and Conservation,* S.A. El-Swaify and associates, eds. Ankeney, Iowa: Soil Conservation Society of America.

World Resources Institute

1709 New York Avenue, N.W.
Washington, D.C. 20006, U.S.A.

The World Resources Institute (WRI) is a policy research center created in late 1982 to help governments, international organizations, and private business address a fundamental question: How can societies meet basic human needs and nurture economic growth without undermining the natural resources and environmental integrity on which life, economic vitality, and international security depend?

Two dominant concerns influence WRI's choice of projects and other activities:

The destructive effects of poor resource management on economic development and the alleviation of poverty in developing countries; and

The new generation of globally important environmental and resource problems that threaten the economic and environmental interests of the United States and other industrial countries and that have not been addressed with authority in their laws.

The Institute's current areas of policy research include tropical forests, biological diversity, sustainable agriculture, energy, climate change, atmospheric pollution, economic incentives for sustainable development, and resource and environmental information.

WRI's research is aimed at providing accurate information about global resources and population, identifying emerging issues, and developing politically and economically workable proposals.

In developing countries, WRI provides field services and technical program support for governments and non-governmental organizations trying to manage natural resources sustainably.

WRI's work is carried out by an interdisciplinary staff of scientists and experts augmented by a network of formal advisors, collaborators, and cooperating institutions in 50 countries.

WRI is funded by private foundations, United Nations and governmental agencies, corporations, and concerned individuals.

DATE DUE

JUL 2 5 1997			
DE 02 '99			

DEMCO 38-297